William Wye Smith

The Poems of William Wye Smith

William Wye Smith

The Poems of William Wye Smith

ISBN/EAN: 9783744714105

Printed in Europe, USA, Canada, Australia, Japan

Cover: Foto ©Thomas Meinert / pixelio.de

More available books at **www.hansebooks.com**

THE
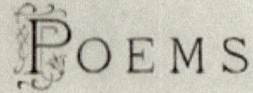POEMS
of
William Wye Smith.

Toronto:
Printed by Dudley & Burns, 11 Colborne Street
1888.

Entered according to Act of the Parliament of Canada, by Rev. WILLIAM WYE SMITH, in the year Eighteen Hundred and Eighty-Eight, in the Office of the Minister of Agriculture, at Ottawa.

CONTENTS.

	PAGE
PREFATORY	7

MISCELLANEOUS—

Circe	9
The Sunset	10
Jennie MacLean	12
The Waking of the Lark	13
Summer Friends	15
Sailing On	16
Why do you Envy Me?	17
The Boy and the Dove	18
Comforted	20
To my Son	21
When Spring in its Glory was come	22
Love and Innocence	24
The New Year	26
Flowers to Bloom in Summers Brighter	27
Under the Rose	28
Indian Summer	29
Fair Leila	30
The Isle of the West	31
The Legend of the Happy Islands	33
The Rainbow	37
Julia	38

CANADIAN—

The Second Concession of Deer	41
Here's to the Land	43
Death of Wolfe	44
Youth and Age	45
O, the Woods	47
When Johnnie went away	49
The Rosebud Early	50

CANADIAN—*Continued.*

The Wild Rose	51
Indian Falls, Owen Sound	52
The Fisherman of Point Pelee	53
The Blue Sea is before Me	54
John Greenwood	56
The Sheep-Washing	58
Sweet Content	60
Strike to the Chalk	61
The Days gone by	62
The Canadians on the Nile	63
The Girl that Drove the Reaper	64
Canadian Winter Song	66
The Violet	69
Think of Me	71
The Merry Maple	72
The Volunteer of '85	73

SCOTTISH—

The Vale of Tweed	77
The Nurse o' Men	81
The Border Poet	82
Peden's Prayer	84
The Bairnie	85
Wee Jeanie	87
The Bonnie Land	88
Robert Fergusson	90
Our Bonnie Bairn's Asleep	91
The Prisoner	92
Loch Saint Mary	84
Habbie Simpson	95
Rab MacQuheen and his Elshin	100
Hame Again	105
Bonnie Eneuch	107
Wallace Wight	108
James Guthrie	109
The Martyr of Solway Sands	111

CONTENTS. iii

SCOTTISH—*Continued.*

Robert Bruce 113
Thomas the Rhymer 115
Wallace's Farewell to Marion 116
Burns 118
Our Hame is whaur we mak our Nest 120
Craws 124
The Highland Laddie 132
Wi' the Laverock i' the Lift 133
Bessie Bell and Mary Gray 134
The Broom of the Cowdenknowes 136
Fare thee Weel .... 13.
Will ye tak me 139
The gay Goss-hawk 140
Louie Campbell 141
Bring a Wheen Laverocks 142
The Bush aboon Traquair 144
The Ghost that Danced at Jethart 145
Gin ye canna gie the Pund 150
The Birdie that's wantin' a Wing 151

RELIGIOUS—

I came, but I came with Myself 155
The Merits of Christ for Nothing 156
The Cross-Bearer 157
Come, O come, thou King Eternal 159
Better than all 160
I had one for an Enemy 161
When you get Home 162
My Heavenly Friend 163
Bethel 164
The Song of Moses 165
God of Glory 166
Christ the only Priest 167
Moses 168
The Mount of Vision 169
Israel Crossing Jordan 170

RELIGIOUS—*Continued.*

Go seek a Man in Bethlehem	173
Keep me Free and Pure	174
Elijah	175
The Lepers	177
Building for God	178
The Curse of Wine	179
Awake, awake, O Zion	180
God Restoring	181
Earth's Jubilee	182
Temptations	184
Blessed	185
The Lord's Prayer	186
The Two Ways	186
House on the Rock	187
There's a Boat has Launched Away	188
Come to the Saviour Now	189
Transfigured	190
At the Treasury	191
True Repentance	192
Holy Saviour, Heavenly Bread	193
Go forth, go forth, ye chosen	194
The Lepers	195
Jesus Risen	196
Now, now	197
The Glad News	198
Saul of Tarsus	199
Thou must keep Me	200
Half Persuaded	201
A Scotch Paraphrase	202
I hear the Word	203

PSALMS—

The Godly—Ps. I	207
The Coming of the King—Ps. II	208
The Faithful Friend—Ps. XII	209
The Creator's Power—Ps. XXIX	210

Psalms—*Continued.*

Confession and Pardon—Ps. XXXII	212
Following Hard—XLII	214
The City of the Great King—Ps. XLVIII	216
"My Heart is Fixed."—Ps. LVII	218
The Sheltering Rock—Ps. LXI	220
Christ's Dominion—Ps. LXXII	221
The Courts of the Lord—Ps. LXXXIV	222
The City of Our God—Ps. LXXXVII	224
Our Almighty Friend—Ps. XCV	225
Exalted Praise—Ps. CXIII	226
A Plaint—Ps. CXX	227
The City of God—Ps. CXXII	228
Aid Implored—Ps. CXXIII	229
An Anthem—Ps. CXXIV	230
God's Protection—Ps. CXXV	231
Out of Captivity—Ps. CXXVI	232
The Blessing of the Saint—Ps. CXXVII	233
Suffering—Ps. CXXIX	234
Out of the Depths—Ps. CXXX	235
Humility—Ps. CXXXI	236
Love of Brethren—CXXXIII	236
Blessing—Ps. CXXXIV	237
The Exile's Lament—Ps. CXXXVII	238
The Ever-Present God—Ps. CXXXIX	239
Universal Praise—Ps. CXLVIII	240
Ecstatic Praise—Ps. CVIII	242

Children's Pieces—

The Prince and the Beggar	245
When our Ship Comes in	246
Gather the Flowers	247
Wondrous Star	248
The Ten Commandments	249
The Visitor	248
Seeing Not, Yet Loving	250

CHILDREN'S PIECES—*Continued.*

"Even a Cup of Cold Water." 251
Imperfect 252
The Lintie 253
O my Saviour 255
Blessed Kingdom 256
The Tongue 257
Little White-Head 258
The Cow that ran to Goderich 258
Ten Little Fingers 259
David and Jonathan 260
Sweet to Know 261

Some of the Hymns and other pieces in this volume have become the property of *The Sunday School Times*, Philadelphia; David C. Cook, Chicago; and the Messrs. Dougall, Montreal; and are inserted here by their kind permission.

PREFATORY.

FROM billowed Lakes beneath the Northern star,
That throb against her granite battlements—
To where the Northern Lights hold mystic dance,
Canadia lies, with mellow sunbeams crowned.
'Tis not a storied land of old romance—
For men still battle with the rooted giants
That once held solemn court o'er all the land ;—
And all her Poets are but striplings yet,
And joyous hope the keynote of their hymns.

Yet one of these—not bay, but maple-crowned—
Hath set him down to sing his country's praise.
Not from the windows of the city, viewing
The pride that but affects some other pride
In lands afar, where Mammon hath grown old,
And in his dotage flings his gold about :—
But from the bosky dell and silent wood—
From hill-top crowned with sumach and wild brier,—
From gentle meadows, where the beaver once
Held carnival amid the nameless streams—

From cabins reared of most Titanic trunks,
And roofed and ceiled with cedar, as of old,—
From fields of scented clover, sloping down
Toward some gleaming lakelet in the vale,—
From hidden corner of the tortuous fence,
Amid the wild-flowers, and the long thin grass:—
These are his outlooks, and from these he draws
The inspiration of his rustic song.

Miscellaneous.

CIRCE.

In a beautiful Island dwelt Circe the Fair—
    Child of the Light!
Sea-blue in her eyes, and the sun on her hair,—
    Golden and bright;—
But the terror of those who adventured them there—
    Enchantress and sprite!

For she had been told that from far-distant land,
    O'er the sea foam,
A Hero should cast his light prow on the strand
    Of her sweet Island home;
And at sight of her beauty, and touch of her hand,
    Should nevermore roam!

And though they might come who were noble to see,
    All smiling secure,—
High over all Suitors her Hero should be,
    (Thus the Oracle sure):
For naught of the *brute* in his nature had he—
    Loving and pure.

And so, with this augury always at hand,
    Early and late
She put them to test 'neath her magical wand
    And her goblet of fate;

And, swine if they were, they were swine at command,
    And grunted and ate!

And why should we blame, in her Isle 'mid the brine,
    The Enchantress alone?
If they had been *men*, they had never been swine,—
    Circe or none!
Oh braggart, beware! lest the doom should be thine,
    Ere rising of sun!

For a man to the core is a man that will stand
    To be tested and tried;—
And the bootless enchantments and magical wand
    Are all laid aside:
The True-Hearted comes, and she gives him her hand—
    Hero and Bride!

THE SUNSET.

Banners hung out in the western sky,
Crimson, and golden and purple dye;
Sweet islands to anchor your fancy by,
    As they drift to the lee of the Day:—
Mountains emerging from worlds of bliss,
Yet covered and cradled in snow like *this*—
Yet it cannot be snow, for the sun's warm kiss
    Makes it blush, but it hies not away!

Glory come down with her girdle loose,
To fill it with flowers for Fancy's use,—

And Happiness smiles at the ample truce
    O'er land, and sky and sea ;—
When all things lovely, and fair and bright,
Link hand in hand in their calm delight,
And there's not a heart on the Earth to-night,
    But beats peace to thee and me!

If we *could* but call it some other name,
That spoke not of Earth, or its sin and shame—
A waft of the everlasting fame
    Eternity only can bring—
Then, lover and friend, it were Earth no more,
But an outlying Cape of Eternity's shore!—
For sin only hinders the channel bridged o'er
    That lies between us and our King!

So let our sweet Fancy on furthermost wing,
To return by-and-bye, and an olive-leaf bring,
That belongs to a Land where the birds ever sing,
    And thy joy and thy youth are for aye!
For lands we have fancied and lands we have bought,
With a glance of the mind, and a turn of the thought,—
In our lives interweaved, in our spirits inwrought,
    Shall be ours at the breaking of day!

JENNIE MacLEAN.

Softly we laid thee away to thy rest,
    Jennie MacLean!
Sweet was thy smile, as the flowers on thy breast—
    Far above pain!
Early thy sun went down, yet it was best—
    Jennie MacLean!

"Yes, it was better!" we say, now 'tis past—
    Jennie MacLean!
Heaven was thy home, and Heaven wearied at last,
    To have thee again:—
The haven is reached, and the anchor is cast—
    Jennie MacLean!

Hands folded now that were never at rest,
    Jennie MacLean!
Till the wants of the widow and orphan were blest;—
    And their tears fell like rain,
When they knew that she slept whom they ever loved best—
    Jennie MacLean!

Thus "His beloved He giveth His sleep,"
    Jennie MacLean!
Peaceful as morning, when storms loud and deep
    Sink on the main:—
Earth is the richer thy memory to keep,
    Jennie MacLean!

May 2, 1881.

THE WAKING OF THE LARK.

[This beautiful lyric, by George E. M. Lancaster, I found in Edwards' Modern Scottish Poets; but it seemed to me to lose much of its harmony and beauty, by a rudeness in the ending of each stanza—the last line not rhyming with anything. I have remedied this; and I think, considerably improved the poem by so doing. W. W. S.]

O bonnie bird that in the brake, exultant dost prepare thee
(As poets do whose thoughts are true), for wings that will upbear thee,—
 Oh, tell me, tell me, bonnie bird,
 Canst thou not pipe of hope deferred,
Or canst thou sing of only Spring—these golden meadows near thee?

Methinks a bard—and thou art one—should suit his song to sorrow,
And tell of pain as well as gain, that waits us on the morrow;
 But thou art not a prophet, thou,
 If nought but joy can touch thee now,
If in thy heart no anguished vow, sad recollections borrow!

Oh! I have held my sorrows dear, and felt, though poor and blighted,
The songs we love are those we hear, when love is unrequited;
 But thou wert still the slave of dawn,
 And could not sing till night were gone,
Till o'er the pathway of the fawn the quivering sunbeams lighted.

Thou art the minion of the sun, that rises in his splendor,
And canst not spare for Dian fair the songs that should
attend her.
      The moon, so sad and silver-pale,
      Is mistress of the nightingale,—
But never thou, from hill or dale, canst darkling ditties
send her!

For queen or king thou wilt not spare one note of thine
outpouring,
For thou art free as breezes be, on Nature's velvet flooring.
      The daisy with its hood undone,
      The grass, the sunlight, and the sun,—
These are thy joys, thou holy one, in singing and in
soaring!

O hush! O hush! how wild a gush of rapture in the
distance!
A roll of rhymes, a toll of chimes, a cry for love's assist-
ance:—
      A sound that wells from happy throats,
      A flood of song where beauty floats,
And where thoughts glide like golden boats, on on, with-
out resistance!

This is the advent of the lark, in humble gray apparel,
Who doth prepare to trill in air his sinless summer carol.
      This is the prelude to the lay
      The birds did sing in Homer's day,
And will again, for aye and aye, win praise's sweetest
laurel.

O dainty thing on wonder's wing, to life and love related,
Oh, sing aloud, from cloud to cloud, till day be consecrated;
    Till from the gateways of the morn,
    The sun, with all his light unshorn,
His robes of darkness from him torn, shall scale the
    heavens elated!

SUMMER FRIENDS.

Sweet Summer friends, I would ye were
  Still in my sight as in my heart;
And that no waning Summer e'er
  Could whisper hoarse, Depart, depart!
    For like a flower
    In withered bower,
    Forgot by shower,
    And kissed by frost—
My heart seems in a sunset-land,
  Where all is past and all is lost!

Ye came what time the Summer heard
  'Mid tedded hay the silvan song;
Ye went before the earliest bird
  Was missed from 'mong the tuneful throng—
    And with you went
    My heart's content,
    All idly spent
    And thrown away;
And but the empty casket left,
  Where, once enshrined, a jewel lay.

THE BOY AND THE DOVE.

A little boy went forth at morn,
  With his shout and whistle cheery ;
But bruised by stone, and pierced by thorn,
  With head and feet so weary—
He sate him down by a garden gate,
  And peeped in at a marble fountain,—
His little basket at his feet,
  With berries from the mountain.

And he forgot his naked feet,
  So blistered, torn and weary,
And he forgot the stony path
  Across the mountain dreary ;
For round that brimming fountain's edge
  Two snowy doves were hovering ;
And the boy looked on as though he saw
  Heaven through some misty covering.

" Good eve, sweet lad ! thy heart, I see,
  Is for those blossoms yearning ! "
" Nay," said the boy, " 'tis to the birds
  My thoughts and eyes are turning.
For they can love us ; and their wings
  Are bright as pictured story ;
And they seem to teach me many things
  Of Paradise and glory."

" Then 'tis the lark you would prefer ;
  The boundless blue ascending—

As if from heaven his song he drew,
  And sent it down unending.
Or is the red-breast your delight ?
  That boys, the wide-world over,
Have loved since first the wandering babes
  He happed in leafy cover.

" 'Tis not the lark, nor yet the bird
  So loved in olden story."
" Then 'tis the swallow; round whose name
  Old legends hang a glory.
They say he plucked the cruel thorns
  From the brow of **Jesus** dying ;
And perch'd upon the cross, as though
  That mocking crowd defying."

" I had not thought of that," he said,
  " For I have little learning ;
But I thought the *dove* was most like those
  Who God's love are discerning ;
And then the Holy Ghost chose
  That shape to take at Jordan ;
Descending on the Saviour's head,
  As on our hearts his pardon !"

And so he took his basket up,
  Fillled for his precious mother ;
And I returned with love and hope
  Encouraging each other
Within my heart, to think that we
  Who thus were kindly speaking,
Might seek for dove-like holiness,
  And find it for the seeking !

COMFORTED.

" My day-dreams all are fled—
And with the sainted dead
Are but an echo of the long ago ; "
So said my heart the while,
As outwardly a smile
Threw its thin mantle o'er the inner wo.

But when a friend, whose eyes
Discovered this disguise,
Approached with open hand and kind intent.
Saying, "Come with us and see
The haunt of bird and bee,
The blossom and the flower so wide besrpent."

My heart, drawn from its grief,
Caught at this kind relief ;
A sympathy that breathed upon my brow,—
And fanned the pulses there,
Familiar with despair,
As fans the cool north wind my temples now.

And in the wild-flower's grace,
I studied face to face
The beauty and the bloom Creation wore ;
And from the silent wood,
And the descending flood,
Came a soft whisper as in days of yore :

" To be as truly blest
As yearns thy beating breast,

Thou must, like us, receive what God has given ;
    Nor miss one sunny ray
    That opens up thy way,—
The sun and gloom alike are sent from Heaven !"

TO MY SON.

Too gentle for the ruder winds of earth,
    To chill and wither ;—
Too many tokens of a heavenly birth,
    Not to flee thither ;—
No wish of mine, though it had magic worth,
    Should draw thee hither !

For I am sad amid these damps sublunar,
    But happy thou !
And I shall doubtless wear that peace the sooner
    Upon my brow,
That I am left, like vine behind the pruner,
    Lopp'd in each bough !

Yet oh, my heart goes out in bitter yearning
    For love so lost !
A smouldering fire, whose embers still are burning
    On altar tossed,
That human pride, that only now is learning
    How love is crossed !

O loved and lost ! 'tis thus the lot of all ;—
    The loved are gone !

And lost to circle of the hearth and hall
    The Angel One
That comes to every house ; whom angels call
    Too soon upon !

WHEN SPRING IN ITS GLORY WAS COME.

When Spring in its glory was come,
    And the fields and the forests were gay,
When the psalms of creation no longer were dumb,
    I heard a one pining and say—
" I am weary of Spring and its flowers —
    I am weary of blossom and leaf !
Of sunshiny glimpses and fast-falling showers,—
    O Spring, in thy passage be brief ! "

When Summer came smiling in pride,
    With a sunbeam for sceptre and crown,
" O, would it were Autumn !" one eagerly cried,
    " Or Winter with chiding and frown !
I am weary of smiles without end—
    I am weary of skies ever clear ;
'Tis the cloud makes the sunshine that follows, a
        friend,—
    O Summer, why tarry so here ? "

In Autumn, when forests were sere,
    And the songs of the Summer were done—
When the winds were all wailing the overthrown
        year,

Thus spoke a disconsolate one :—
"I am weary of withered delights—
　I am weary of garners' full store—
Of short dreamy days, and of wild-wailing nights,—
　O Autumn, then linger no more!"

O children of Earth and of Time!
　Vain, vain is the wish or the thought
That the rolling of seasons, or changing of clime,
　Can bring you the peace that is not!
Ye are pining for pleasures to come—
　Ye are weary of pleasures possessed;
Ye have climbed to the cloud on the mountain's full dome,
　And found it but darkness and mist!

There are joys in the springtime of thought,
　When the soul and its pulses are free;
And the fount that was sprung ere life's battle was fought,
　Channels on, channels on to the sea!
From that stream of our earliest faith,
　We may to some Abana flee,*
But gladly we turn, ere the twilight of death,
　To bathe, O thou Jordan, in thee!

---

* "Are not Abana and Pharpar, rivers of Damascus, better than all the waters of Israel?"

LOVE AND INNOCENCE.

I saw one come, within a pearly boat,
    With eye affixed upon that castle fair;
Rowing him gently to a measured note,
    The softest tuning of the moonlight air!
Circling the little Isle with courses three;
And eyes still fixèd where his heart would be.

At length a little casement opened wide;
    And by the moonlight may he faintly see
A snowy arm the briar-rose part aside,
    Soft twining round the mullion tenderly;—
And by the opened pane she sate her down
Who named was Una, of the lily crown.

Then lay he on his oars, when straight he saw
    Her gentle face, albeit dimly seen;—
As Ghebers to the sun devoutly draw,
    Nor love the less for flitting clouds between—
So moonlight snatches of his Eden's light
Were dear to him as dazzled by her sight.

O did my love in heaven's summit glow!
    ('Twas thus he warbled to his listening love;)
That I might fall upon that neck of snow
    Or 'mid those tresses, like a wounded dove
Weary of light and life, yet not to die,
But in those ambushed ringlets ever lie!

O that my love could ever ever flow,
    Like Silsibél, that fountain of delight,

Through lands of Paradise, whose balm-trees grow,—
    And thou should'st sit, like fragrance-breathing
        night,
Smiling with day-beams, on my banks, and see
The birds of paradise come drink of me!

O that my love could flowery shape assume,
    A lily-bell, or sweet wild-rose to lee;
Upon thy sainted bosom there to bloom—
    For never blight could come on thine or thee!
But ever in disguise of flower or bell,
In sweetest fragrance still of love to tell!

And now upon the blanchèd turret's height,
    In queenly beauty stood his Una fair;
And bowed her head in Luna's swimming light,
    To bind the loosened braidings of her hair;—
Dark as the clouds of a mid summer's night,
And prized by all but her they made so bright.

Breathe but a sigh upon the barren air,
    And it shall fall like balm upon my brow!
Or say adventurous love might hope to share
    The presence of the star he worships now!—
Then would I seek of earth no higher bliss,
Deeming the world's joys gathered into this!

Open, sweet love, thy silver-bolted door!—
    Here stayed be, for the portal opened wide;
And silver lamps their blinding radiance pour
    O'er marble step, and pure lake's rush-grown side;

And like enchantment 'mid the brightness came
Soft-luted ditties, woven round his name.

Like one who wakes, and finds his vision true,
   The lonely rower of the moonlight lake
His slender prow upon the Islet threw,
   As if he feared the charmèd dream might break !—
Upon the terraced marble bounded light,
And vanished in those winding mazes bright.

Turning upon its hinges musical,
   The door has closed upon the wide still world ;
And whispered softly with melodious fall,
   While moonbeams shone, and waters rippling
      curled—
O'er the clear lake and from the pile above—
   "LOVE DWELLS WITH INNOCENCE, AND SHE WITH
      LOVE."

THE NEW YEAR.

Time is like a restless river,
   Bearing on its tide away
Wrecks of radiant hopes, that ever
   Bloom, and fade with closing day.
Bearing on the youth to manhood,
   Bearing manhood past its prime ;—
Changing all things, resting never—
   Touch, oh touch us gently, Time !

We who speak, and ye who **ponder**,—
   We who write and ye who read—
Gliding swiftly down, may wonder
   If we're growing **old** indeed?
If the past **is** gone forever?
   If the present **may not stay**?
Or to-morrow be the giver
   Of the joys we missed to-day?

One year more of all the number
   Given us for our earthly stay,
Gone into the past, where slumber
   Every wasted yesterday!
Up to action! let the present
   Day, and year, and hour of time
Prove, while love and hope are pleasant,
   DUTY ONLY IS SUBLIME!

"FLOWERS TO BLOOM IN SUMMERS BRIGHTER."

SONG.

Why should Summer e'er remember
In this dreary dark December,
When this deadly chill hath bound her,
All the flowers that bloomed around her.
Cold and **low their** bells are sleeping,
Icy tears their only weeping—

Yet does Hope, the stealthy comer,
Whisper of a coming Summer.
> *Flowers to bloom in Summers brighter ;—*
> *Joys to come to hearts made lighter ;—*
> *Sweeter flowers and hopes more joyous—*
> *Till the past no more annoy us !*

Why should Love, with eager sorrow,
Grief from old Remembrance borrow ?
Love is blind, and leads us blindly,—
Deepest love still met unkindly ;—
All the past too fondly waking
Fills the homeless heart to breaking !—
Yet does Hope, the stealthy comer,
Whisper of a flowery Summer.

  Cho.

UNDER THE ROSE.

When Love went a begging, I took the boy in,
 For his quiver was gone, and he pleaded his woes ;
And dreading no danger where none there had been,
 I made him a welcome guest, under the rose.

I told him, as friend to a friend might impart,
 Of a yellow-haired maiden that broke my repose ;
Of the love in her smile, and the scorn in her heart,—
 And he smiled as he counselled me, under the rose.

But treachery lurked in his smile of deceit;
  And the friend that I trusted is leagued with my foes;
The heart is not his, where he boasted his seat;
And the heart that is breaking, is under the rose!

INDIAN SUMMER.

The air is full of sunshine,
  The woods are full of dew;
The lake is like the distant sky,
  The sky has lost its blue;—
And flooded with a golden haze,
  All nature lies becalmed;
Like music in the memory
  With loving thoughts embalmed.
    Stay, stay, sweet Indian Summer!
      I grieve to have thee go!
    O let thy smile be mine awhile,
      'Twixt the Autumn and the snow!

The birds that round my window
  Their early matins sung,—
The flowers I watched each Summer eve,
  Till night its shadows flung;—
And gentle friends that came too late,
  And coming, went to soon—
These all pass o'er my memory
  Like shadows o'er yon moon.
    Cho:

But Nature all is golden,
    Ev'n in her last decay ;
And Hope, that saw its brighter hours
    Will have a happier day.
And love, and friends to crown that love,
    I yet shall live to see ;
Though darkness, distance, winter lies
    Between that hope and me !
Cho :

FAIR LEILA.

I would that I were a flow'ret fair,
  To be plucked by her dainty hands ;
Or twined in the maze of her golden hair,
  As like a sweet dream she stands !
So, many might come, and as many might go,
  Her pride and her beauty to see ;—
How soon she forgot them, I'd care not, nor know,
  But I'd know that she thought upon me !

I would that I were a warbling bird,
  With a song so sweet and clear,
That she needs must pause on the banks of Ouse,
  My carolling voice to hear ?
So, lovers could talk, or lovers be mute,
  But this I could plainly see,
That she turned from them all with a weary look,
  To listen in smiles to me !

I would that I were a murmuring stream,
  That steals through the woods apace,—
To look in her eyes when she softly bends
  To mirror her lovely face.
So, who for a glance of love might sue,
  From under those lashes rare—
I'd mirror myself in Leila's eyes,
  And dwell in contentment there!

But neither a flower, a bird, nor stream,
  Am I; nor ever can be;—
I'm but a herd-boy, in a coat of gray,
  And she's like a Queen to see!
But if it could be, it were hearts alone
  That made us to be or to do,
Fair Leila might yet be all my own,
  And all my dreams be true!

THE ISLE OF THE WEST.

How fair was the day when green Erin had birth,—
The gift that was brightest of Ocean to Earth!
As smiling she lay on the rim of the sea,
Saying, "Come ye oppress'd, and find refuge in me!"

The stranger from far sought the Isle of the West,—
The needy found bread, and the weary found rest;
And green grew her fields in the smile of the sun,
As the hearts of her children were mingled in one!

Och, Erin Aroon ! could my tears but restore
That morning of bliss in the bright days of yore,
I could weep till my heart were dissolved as the rain,
That breaks into blooms as it sinks on the plain.

Yet bright to the gaze of our languishing eyes
Thy heroes of old from the shadows arise :—
Gathelus again, and his followers, throng
The shores they made sacred to learning and song :—

On the field of Clontarf rises Brian Borow—
King Dermot repulses the yellow-haired foe :—
And Erin's Apostle brings light from on high,
Till the Shamrock grows green as the sun-burst goes by !

We watch at the beacons with brave Finn MacCoil,
To stem the invader who touches thy soil ;—
We melt at the music that tells of thy fame—
The Geraldine's beauty—O'Brien's great name.

With sages, and poets with minstrelsy sweet,
We twine a bright garland to lay at thy feet ;
And every green vale shall with echoes prolong
Thy *Caed milla Fealthe* to Genius and Song !

O Mother of Nations ! to lighten thy sigh
How gladly we'd live, and how gladly we'd die !
As fondly, from pages that picture the past
We learn to be one and united at last !

In my heart is a garden no stranger hath known,
And Country and Love are there blooming alone ;

And who loves sweet Erin, whate'er else he be,
Henceforth is a friend and a brother to me!

Then fair be the flow'rets that round thee arise!
And sweet the lark's matin that's sung in thy skies!
As still with thy name in our hearts like a spell,
We waft, broken-hearted, a loving farewell!

THE LEGEND OF THE HAPPY ISLANDS.

The following is the shape the Legend of the Happy Islands takes, among the Algonquins of Algoma. Nanaboosh, otherwise Nanabozo, is the same with Hiawatha. Longfellow however, in celebrating the great primeval Brothers—not having been among the Indians himself, and depending on Schoolcraft's pages—mispronounces, as I take it, the name of the younger brother; the rhythm of the line requires it to be pronounced Chibiábos, with the accent on the third syllable: I never heard it pronounced otherwise among the Indians than Chebáyaboss, with the accent on the *second* syllable of the name.

Back to the days Ojibway legends tell,
When Heroes dwelt where human weaklings dwell!
And Nanaboosh, Prometheus of the van,
Serenely smiled, Father and Friend of man.
The Thinker sate within his Hero's tent—
The Hunter to the hills and forests went.
Great Nanaboosh the human race preserves;
Chebayaboss, as younger brother, serves.
Warned by the Hero to return at dusk,

He duly came with game, and furs, and musk :
Nor trusted once the treacherous frozen lake,
But swept broad circles for his Brother's sake.
Thus the Great Brethren at Creation's birth—
Ere Death or Crime had reaped the shuddering earth !

Down 'mong the demons an uneasy moan
Proclaimed how hateful had this concord grown ;—
And, homeward speeding with o'erladen sledge,
Chebayaboss was found within the edge
Of lake forbidden, and was swallowed there—
White-Lion's victim, and the World's despair.
Then shook with mighty sobs the watery heaven,
And floods descended from the welkin riven,—
Rivers their beds in trembling fear forsook,
And rocks and mountains to their centre shook—
As for his dead the mighty Hero wept ;
And Heaven and Earth a pitying vigil kept.

Fountains may dry ; the Summer comes and goes ;
But grief like this no charmed reversion knows :—
And now as swept the chariot-wheels of Time,
Nor saw cessation of his grief sublime,
The cowering beasts in wild array convene,
From plain, and mount, and lake, and forest green.
The shaggy bison from the breezy plain—
The moose, with many an antler in his train,—
The beaver wise, the bear sedate and slow,
The crouching wolf, the much-consulting crow ;—
And waterfowl, on swift and clamorous wing,
With thousand warblers of the welcome Spring—
And all the gods that heave the floor of Earth,

(There doomed to darkness for their deeds' unworth.)
With them assembled, claim the listening ear
Of Manitou, whom brave and good revere ;—
And plead these wild commotions all might cease,
And Manitou with Nanaboosh make peace.

Who hath not welcomed, from the couch of pain,
A friend, a brother, to his arms again ?
As if Heaven's gate unfolded to our cry,
And gave the friend for whom ourselves would die:
So sate the Hero, as the shadows fell,
And saw Chebayaboss come slowly up the dell !

O Hope ! fallacious most of Fancy's flowers !
As if expended joys could still be ours !
For backward howsoe'er the glance be cast,
Wide yawns the gulf between us and the past !
So Nanaboosh—the first wild welcome o'er—
Wept as he thought of what could be no more !
" O Brother ! " thus he cried, " hadst thou but kept
My equal law, my tears had been unwept.
But now these falling floods have learned to flow,
Deep shall they channel through a world of wo !
Since thou in youth hast sought the grisly shade,
Young and most fair shall all our kindred fade.
In troops they follow in thy forward track,
Nor one fair face, except in dreams, comes back !
But go, my Brother, to the widening West—
Away, away, beyond the mountains' crest—
Beyond the billowed Lakes, that throb in vain—
Beyond the peaks that frown upon the main,—

'Mid calmer waters, never tempest-tossed—
Where Summer flowers are never kissed by frost—
Where greener Isles lie lapped in perfect peace—
Where war, and wo, and death itself shall cease;—
There go, and for thy brethren find a place!—
Thou first in wo, thou Fairest of thy Race!"

Within his brother's eyes he looked a space,—
A long long gaze upon his wo-worn face;
Then turned without a word, and slowly blent
With deepening shadows as he downward went.
And now, whene'er a youthful warrior lies,
And gasps and gazes in his agonies,
They whispering tell, "Chebayaboss has come,
And looked within his eyes to call him home!"
Or when a maiden leaves her mother's side,
With eyes soft sealed, in Death's embrace a bride—
They say her spirit, far beyond the waves,
Has gone to dress the food the Hero craves.

"O silent shore!" 'tis thus the maidens sigh,
"To gain thy bliss how happy could we die!
Where peaceful pillowed rests the weary head,
And fadeless flowers bloom for the early dead:—
Where strife and sorrow nevermore are known,
And the Great Spirit's smile is bliss alone!
Say, brothers, shall we seek that softer strand—
The Happy Islands of the Spirit Land?
And shall we not its blessing bear in part
'Mid all our tears, if we but cleanse the heart!
For the Great Spirit, doubtless, loves to see
His children *now* what then they wish to be!"

THE RAINBOW.

They say there is gold where the rainbow rests,
    And often I ran for to find it ;—
But the meadows were gay, and the flowers on my way
    Whispered all to me never to mind it !
The rainbow ran down 'twixt the brook and the tree,
I could see it as plainly as plainly could be,—
But when I got there it was some other tree,
    And not where I thought I should find it !

      But the rainbow was there, in the heart bright
          and fair,
      If only I'd looked for it rightly !
      But the rainbow was there in the heart bright
          and fair,
      If only I'd looked for it rightly !

No longer a boy, 'tis the rainbow no more
    That mocks all my fondest endeavour ;
But friendships grow cold, and my joys worn and old,
    And happiness misses me ever !
I'll tell you a scheme—but it's 'twixt you and me—
I shall let selfish joy and my " happiness " be,—
And live for redressing the woes that I see,
    And think of self never, Oh never !

      But the rainbow was there, in the heart bright
          and fair,
      As soon as I looked for it rightly !
      But the rainbow was there, in the heart bright
          and fair,
      As soon as I looked for it rightly !

JULIA.

Pure as the lily that bloomed on her breast,
   Silent she lies with the world at her feet;—
Beauty in marble—serenely at rest—
      Transfigured, and sweet!

Hebe-like fulness—no waste nor decay—
   Fair rounded forehead, prophetic of power;
Thought there unfolding, like roses in *May*—
      The buds of the hour!

Closed the dark eyes, where in meekness and truth
   She looked on a world where a foe she had none;
Their light faded out ere the noontide of youth,—
      But 'tis glory begun!

One lesson learned—of all learning the best—
   Who would be blest, to the Blessed must come!
Opened the arms that would fold her to rest—
      Welcomed, at Home!

There would we leave her, our darling and pride;
   The flower of His garden, the Master has won!
She blooms now in Eden; and there glorified,
      She beckons us on!

CANADIAN.

"Will nobody write a few songs for Canada?"

THOMAS MACQUEEN.

Canadian.

THE SECOND CONCESSION OF DEER.

JOHN Tompkins lived in a house of logs,
   On the second concession of Deer;
The front was logs, all straight and sound—
The gable was logs, all tight and round—
The roof was logs, so firmly bound—
And the floor was logs, all down to the ground—
   The warmest house in Deer.

And John, to my mind, was a log himself,
   On the second concession of Deer;—
None of your birch, with bark of buff—
Nor basswood, weak and watery stuff—
But he was hickory, true and tough,
And only his outside bark was rough;—
   The grandest old man in Deer!

But John had lived too long, it seemed,
   On the second concession of Deer!
For his daughters up the governing rein,
With a fine brick house on the old domain,
All papered, and painted with satinwood stain,
Carpeted stairs, and best ingrain—
   The finest house in Deer!

Poor John, it was sad to see him now,
    On the second concession of Deer!
When he came in from his weary work,
To strip off his shoes like a heathen Turk,—
Or out of the *company's* way to lurk,
And ply in the *shanty* his knife and fork—
        The times were turned in Deer!

But John was hickory to the last,
    On the second concession of Deer!
And out on the river-end of his lot,
He laid up the logs in a cosy spot,
And self and wife took up with a cot,
And the great brick house might swim or not—
        He was done with the pride of Deer!

But the great house could not go at all,
    On the second concession of Deer;
'Twas *mother* no more, to wash or bake,
Nor *father* the gallants' steeds to take—
From the kitchen no more came pie nor cake—
And even their butter they'd first to make!—
        There were lessons to learn in Deer!

And the lesson they learned a year or more,
    On the second concession of Deer;—
Then the girls got back the brave old pair—
And gave the mother her easy chair—
She told them how, and they did their share—
And John the honors once more did wear
        Of his own domain in Deer!

HERE'S TO THE LAND!

Here's to the Land of the rock and the pine:
    Here's to the Land of the raft and the river!
Here's to the Land where the sunbeams shine,
    And the night that is bright with the North-light's quiver!

Here's to the Land of the axe and the hoe!
    Here's to the hearties that give them their glory;—
With stroke upon stroke, and with blow upon blow,
    The might of the forest has passed into story!

Here's to the Land with its blanket of snow,—
    To the hero and hunter the welcomest pillow!
Here's to the land where the stormy winds blow
    Three days, ere the mountains can talk to the billow!

Here's to the buckwheats that smoke on her board!
    Here's to the maple that sweetens their story:—
Here's to the scythe that we swing like a sword,—
    And here's to the fields where we gather our glory!

Here's to her hills of the moose and the deer;
    Here's to her forests, her fields and her flowers!
Here's to her homes of unchangeable cheer,
    And the maid 'neath the shade of her own native bowers!

DEATH OF WOLFE.

High on the rocky crest
   We formed in still array;
And knee to knee we stood at rest,
   And waited for the day.
Till from each tower and trench
   The warning bugles rung;
And soon the banners of the French
   Upon the breeze were flung.

And firing, down they swept
   With stern attacking art:
While we a dreadful silence kept,
   Till each could hear his heart.
" Now *fire!*" cried Wolfe, and when
   Our sudden thunder broke,
It seemed far off to listening men
   Like bolt that rends the oak.

He waved his shattered hand,
   And pointed to the foe;
When ran along the British band
   The cheer that Britons know!
Ah, who could tell that he
   That gallant charge who led,
Should blend our shouts of victory
   With wailings for the dead!

He followed with his eyes,
    As we kept thundering on ;
And when we came to claim the prize,
    His praise for victory won—
They told us, 'neath their breath,
    Our youthful Hero slept !—
The battle-field his couch of death,—
    His praise his country kept.

YOUTH AND AGE.

He sat upon a mossy stone,
    Beside the river's brim—
And wondered why the rapturous scene
    No raptures had for him !
The creeping willows lined the banks,
    The flowers stood tall and fair—
And o'er his head the poplar leaves
    Were beckoning to the air.

He summoned up his vanished youth
    To breathe once more the bliss—
For never had his eyes beheld
    A brighter scene than this !
Where was the spirit, that of yore
    Kindled at such a theme—
And wove poetic fancies
    In the texture of his dream ?

The river babbled in its glee—
    A babe that ne'er grew old ;
And near, the spiry golden-rod
    Played with its plumes of gold :—
'Twas not in these—'twas in himself
    That fire and fancy slept !
And there, beside Yamaska's wave
    The old man sate and wept.

"Come back, come back, my youth !" he cried,
    " And live one glowing hour :
And let my heart once more dilate
    At Nature's sweetest power !
Come, clothe these banks with greener trees,
    Each flower with fairer hue,—
And tint the overarching skies
    With deeper dyes of blue !

Give to the song of every bird
    The ' added line ' of bliss ;
And let the world of fancy teem
    Its stores to add to this :—
Let autumn never sweep these fields—
    These skies ne'er tempest-crossed—
Nor let this summer greenery
    Be ever kissed by frost !"

Ah, pilgrim to the sunny banks
    Of bright Yamaska's stream !
For all the decadence of age,
    Thou still canst sweetly dream !

'Tis Heaven, not Earth, thou'st pictured so,—
    And thus it comes to be,
That glory from the coming day
    Breaks on the day we see.

We leave behind the best of Earth,
    Adown the darkened past;
And upward, with the brightening day,
    We press to peace at last.
And often find that glory mix
    With scenes we earthly deem—
As with the bard who musing sate
    Beside Yamaska's stream.

SONG: O, THE WOODS!

O, the woods, the woods! the leafy woods,
    And the laughing face of Spring!
When the birds return from their far sojourn,
    With their latest new songs to sing!
Then let me hie to the leafy woods,
    And banish my woe and care—
O, I'll never repent of the day I went,
    To learn a sweet lesson there!

O, the woods, the woods! the Summer woods,
    And the coolness of their shade!
Where in wildwood dell all the Graces dwell,
    There to wait on a sylvan maid!

I'll seek for flowers to deck her bowers,
 And twine in her golden hair ;
And I wonder much if she thinks of such
 As I, when the Winter's there?

O, the woods, the woods! the Autumn woods,
 And the chestnuts ripe and brown !
When the leaves hang bright in the changing light,
 Like the banners of old renown !
And South-winds ripple across the lake,
 Like chiming of marriage-bells ;—
O, I wouldn't much grieve, if I'd never leave
 These wildest of woodland dells !

O, the woods, the woods ! Canadia's woods,
 And the sweet flowers nourished there !
O, the beechen shade, and the sylvan maid
 That garlands her golden hair !
Her name may change with the magic ring—
 Her heart is the same for aye !—
In my little canoe there is room for two,
 And sweetly we glide away !

SONG: WHEN JOHNNIE WENT AWAY.

The waters warbled down the dell,
   Their wintry bands untwining,—
And mottled shadows softly fell
   From ancient elms reclining.
The wind-flower waked to see the sky,
Where tender blue the violets lie,
'Neath budding beeches waving high—
   When Johnnie went away.

The early birds returned to sing
   The songs they had been singing;
And o'er the hills the hand of Spring
   A royal robe was flinging:—
A glory fell from upper air,
O'er river-marge and meadows fair;—
And song and fragrance everywhere—
   When Johnnie went away.

The Spring was gone, and with her went
   Those blossoms, ne'er returning;
And, all the fires of Summer spent,
   Our hearts grew sad and yearning.
The withered wealth of forests lay
On Quinté's hills in death's decay,
And gloomy closed the shortening day,
   When Johnnie came again!

The rain came down; it seemed like tears
    Of joy at his returning;
As backward, through the mist of years,
    We saw that Spring sun burning!
The flowers sprang up in memory's train,
We heard once more the sylvan strain—
Our Spring has all come back again,
    With Johnnie safe at home!

SONG: THE ROSEBUD EARLY.

I planted a rose by my garden bower,
    A rose that blossomed rarely;
And I said, as I watched it hour by hour,
    "I'll give him a rosebud early!"

The Spring sun warmed to Summer's heat,
    And flowers were bursting fairly,
When I heard the drums at midnight beat,
    And the ranks were forming early.

Of days that passed I counted four,
    While a solemn sun shone clearly,—
When a horseman brought to my father's door
    A withered rosebud early.

I asked not why the foeman comes?
    Or who the day won fairly?—
But I knew nine fell 'mid the clover blooms,
    And one with a rosebud early.

His sisters mourn in weeds of woe,
    For a brother loved so dearly ;—
I may not tell what none must know,
    But I cherish that rosebud early !

O weary now the hours I tell
    Of my day that broke so clearly ;—
For its light went out when at Ridgeway fell
    The youth with the Rosebud early !

SONG: THE WILD ROSE.

O sweetest of our wildings,
    Thou hast not come too soon !
I've waited for thee longingly,
    These many days of June ;—
Yet not so many as they seem,
    For thou didst make them long :—
Thou sweetest of our wildings,
    Thy loveliness is song !

I watched thy buds expanding,
    As day by day they grew ;
Till five sweet leaves of beauty rare
    Disclosed their blushing hue.
My heart grew jealous of its love,
    I placed thee on my breast ;—
I watched thy buds expanding !
    Could'st thou deny the rest ?

Another day of blooming,
   If I had touched thee not !
'Twas love that took thyself away,
   Lest thou shouldst be forgot !
So unto many a flower we say
   Whom PARADISE hath won—
" Another day of blooming—
   But—farther from the sun ! "

Nor shalt thou be forgotten
   When all thy leaves are dead ;
A sweet perfume is sensible,
   That lingers in thy stead.
So may some heart, with tears perchance,
   Repeat when I am gone—
" Nor shalt *thou* be forgotten,
   Thou sad and lonely one ! "

INDIAN FALLS, OWEN SOUND.

A placid stream without a name,
   That wandered eastward through the shade,
To a dread brink all sudden came,
   And madly leaped, a wild cascade.
And onward through the thickening gloom,
   It now pursues its troubled way,
Until its waters find their tomb
   Within the depths of Newash Bay.

Beneath the sheet adventurous eyes
    May see **bright** rainbows in the stream;
And on each **rock** that pictured lies
    Quivers the fervid noontide beam.
Fit haunt, beneath some lowering beech,
    Or the wych-hazel in **the dell,**
For youthful hearts to learn and **teach**
    The dawning witchery **of love's spell!**

And like that stream, some youthful heart
    Glides calmly o'er life's golden **sand,**
Until awaked by passion's start,
    It rushes headlong to the strand.
Sweet **Fall!** in thee I oft shall **trace**
    Disjointed memories **known before;**
And in thine eddies see my **face**
    Calm as of old—but glad no more!

SONG: THE FISHERMEN OF POINT PELEE

    I looked upon **Lake Erie,**
        Before I looked on thee;
    And I'll not leave it for thy **gold**
        That lies beyond the sea!
    Its **waves** come leaping to my **hand,**
        As if they feared I'd go—
    I look upon Lake Erie,
        And my heart gives answer, "No!"

Upon the shores of Erie
　My cradle-song was sung :
And round its coves and o'er its deeps
　My childish shoutings rung ;—
Nor think my heart can e'er forget
　The old love and the true—
Upon the shores of Erie,
　That round its magic threw.

Thou bid'st me seek some other land
　Away beyond the line,
Where gold is like the river sand,
　And spice grows like the pine ;—
I hear it ; but my native strand
　Has earned so well my love,
That when I seek some other land
　'Twill be a land Above !

SONG : THE BLUE SEA IS BEFORE ME.

The blue sea is before me,
　And behind Canadia's strand ;—
Farewell, farewell the valleys
　Of my own dear western land !
Though friendly eyes and voices
　May greet me where I roam,
There's no friend's like the tried friends
　I leave behind at home.

Ye idle winds that wander
    This watery waste above,
O carry with you homeward
    A kiss to her I love!
Nor whisper whence the token came,
    Nor ask me who is she?
Go find the fairest fair one—
    She's dreaming of the sea!

In thought I'm 'mid the lilies,
    And the violets, tender blue,
Beneath the oak and chestnut,
    With the broad lake peeping through!
Where the tardy-robing sumach,
    And the beech's shady noon,
Bespeak the opening glories
    Of our bright Canadian June!

Had I the pearls of Ocean,
    Or the gems beneath our lee,
To speak my heart's devotion
    In a diadem for thee —
'Twere worthier, but not more sincere
    Than now I waft a-lee,
A prayer for dear Canadia,
And a blessing, love, for thee!

JOHN GREENWOOD.

John Greenwood lived by Scugog lake —
    (The waters were clear, and the skies were blue ;)
And John was willing to give and take,
    (And the woods and waters were fair to view !)
His sons were reared at a free fire-side,—
    With little of learning, and nothing of pride,—
But many a lesson of backwoods lore
    He gave, as his sire had given before,
When they sauntered in as the horn did blow—
    Fond hoping that some of the seed would grow !

Now said those sons at Scugog lake —
    (The waters were clear, and the skies were blue ;)
"Whatever the world will give, we'll take !"
    (And the woods and waters were fair to view !)
And Harry left the old roof-tree,
    For the golden land by the Western Sea ;—
"No room beneath these Northern skies,
    For one who would grasp at a glittering prize !"
And friends he found, both loud and frank,
Who spoke in slang, and called him "Hank !"

And Ned would leave sweet Scugog's side—
    (The waters were clear, and the skies were blue ;)
"In the ranks of Commerce his place he'd take !"
    (And the woods and waters were fair to view !)
The "gee-buck trade" he held in scorn,
    And mocked at the place where he was born ;

To speak with a simper, and sport a ring,
    Part hair in the middle, and walk with a spring,
We're all in the way to his coveted fame,
    And added " Esquire " at the end of his name.

But Lawrence lived by Scugog lake—
    (The waters were clear, and the skies were blue ;)
What grew in the fertile fields he'd take—
    (And the woods and waters were fair to view !)
His hands grew strong, and his head grew clear,
    His wife was fair, and his babes were dear—
He envied none, for his lot was blest
    With bread and to spare, and a heart at rest,
As he sate in the rays of the sinking sun,
    And looked back at the day with its duties done.

John Greenwood lived by Scugog lake—
    (The waters were clear, and the skies were blue ;)
As ready as ever to give and take ;
    (And the woods and waters were fair to view !)
And Harry came back from wasted wealth,
    Weak in his pocket, and weak in his health ;
And Ned, who had gone to the wall in trade,
    Came back to the dear old homestead's shade ;
And John looked up, with a smile in store—
" My boys are all back who are boys no more !

" We'll bid farewell to Scugog lake,"
    (The waters were blue, and the skies were clear ;)
" And back to the bush our way we'll take !"
    (And the woods and waters were fair to view !)

Now each one tills his widening fields,
    Where the forest gloom to the sunlight yields;
Neighbor, and brother, and sire and son,—
    A "Greenwood" township has begun!
For in here broad lap, old mother earth
    Carries no idlers, and knows no dearth!

THE SHEEP-WASHING.

My heart is glad to-night—
    Too glad for a wink of sleep!
For Jenny has promised to be my bride
    As soon as we wash the sheep!
And I don't care how soon I see them
    Plunging in and out of the creek;
For a sweeter young wife for a farmer
    Than Jenny, I could not seek.

But someway, I don't half like it—
    It may come either late or soon;
And a raw cold spring may put off the thing
    Away till the middle of June!
I wish she had set a day
    That we could delight to keep!
Some old Saint's day, or the First of May,
    That had nothing to do with sheep!

But she set down her foot so firmly—
"There was so *much work* to do—
And my father," she knew, " couldn't spare
    the team
  Till all the spring-work was through!"
That I couldn't say much to her,
  To shorten my heart's suspense,—
Especially as I lost my hold
  Of the stake-and-rider fence!

And then, as I gained my feet—
  (And she didn't seem a bit scared,
She said, "She knew I'd fall soft,
  And the damage was easy repaired!")
She got the idea of wool-picking—
  Perhaps from the clay in my hair,
And she said, "When ours was ready to sort,
  To tell the girls she'd *be there!*"

I can't change Jenny, I warrant;
  Nor would I risk aught, like a fool;
So I'm wishing for first-rate weather,
  And a rise in the price of *wool!*
But you who have weddings in prospect,
  Don't o'er the arrangements sleep;
Nor ever let such a particular time
  Depend on the washing of sheep!

I'll make my father believe
  He's losing half of his wool;
That the bushes have all begun to thieve,
  And the thorns are hanging full!

  I'll hurry the matter up,
   And give the Cotswolds a steep!
  The hardy fellows—they'll stand it well!
   We shant be last with our sheep!

SONG: SWEET CONTENT.

I live in a town where the sun shines round,
 And the hills behind are green;
Where a sweet stream falls with a musical sound,
 And where many a flower is seen!
And the gardens fair are open to all,
 And the fruits hang golden there;
And there's never a joy to the richest fall,
 But the poorest may freely share.

Do you know the town? Have you heard its renown?
 Its name is sweet "Content!"
And the way to it lies just before your eyes—
 The way the happy went!

The landscapes so fair in the clouds above
 May be found in the fields below;
And the winds that breathe seem to whisper of love,
 In the Summer-evening glow;
And the music swells from palace and cot,
 As the twilight turns to gloom;
And if there's a wish that the heart finds not,
 There's a pleasure to take its room!
CHO:

SONG: STRIKE TO THE CHALK.

It may be a log you cut—
   Or a false friend it may be;
Or an evil habit you score away,
   Or it may be a tree!

      Strike to the chalk, my boys!
      Strike, strike away!
      Even let the flying chips
      Hit whom they may!

A man, like a noble pine,
   May be straight as duty's mark;
Yet they both have need of the hewer's line
   To score the useless bark!
CHO:

You might do aright, my friend;
   Or the right may be with me;
But be sure you follow the scorer's line
   Thy conscience marks for thee!
CHO:

A chalk line for every man;
   And a chalk line for the tree!
And I won't feel hurt if the scorer's axe
   Should follow the chalk with me!
CHO:

SONG: THE DAYS GONE BY.

A star for you, and a star for me,
    And a star in the summer sky ;
And we named them there,
By the Lake so fair,
    In the days gone by !

    O, the days gone by !
    The days gone by !
O'er memory's track how the heart goes back
    To the days gone by !

My star is still in the brow of Night,
    And the star of your love shines high :
But we walk no more,
On that bright lake's shore,
    As in days gone by !
Cho :

There's change and chance, and there's many
       a storm
    Has o'erclouded our early sky ;
And we wander on,
In the way we've gone—
    From the days gone by !
Cho :

Yet many an hour does my fancy flee
    To the lake and the Summer sky,
And that early vow
That is sweet even now—
    In the days gone by !
Cho :

SONG: THE CANADIANS ON THE NILE.

O, the East is but the West, with the sun a little hotter;
And the pine becomes a palm, by the dark Egyptian water:
And the Nile's like many a stream we know, that fills its brimming cup;
We'll think it is the Ottawa, as we track the batteaux up!
  Pull, pull, pull! as we track the batteaux up!
  It's easy shooting homeward, when were at the top!

O, the cedar and the spruce, line each dark Canadian river;
But the thirsty date is here, where the sultry sunbeams quiver;
And the mocking mirage spreads its view, afar on either hand;
But strong we bend the sturdy oar, towards the Southern land!
Cho:

O, we've tracked the Rapids up, and o'er many a portage crossing;
And it's often such we've seen, though so loud the waves are tossing!
Then, it's homeward when the run is o'er! o'er stream, and ocean deep—
To bring the memory of the Nile, where the maple shadows sleep!
Cho:

And it yet may come to pass, that the hearts and hands
    so ready
May be sought again to help, when some poise is off the
    steady !
And the Maple and the Pine be matched, with British
    Oak the while,
As once beneath Egyptian suns, the Canadians on the
    Nile !
Cho :

THE GIRL THAT DROVE THE REAPER.

    It was by the quiet Credit,—
      Not a wing nor leaf was stirred,
    And the whirring of the Reaper
      Was the only sound I heard.
    And through the envious bushes
      That o'erhung the space between,
    I espied a gipsy bonnet,
      With a fluttering bow of green.

    Then I spurred a little onward,
      And I doffed my ready hat ;
    For there with royal presence
      On a very throne she sat,—
    With a riding-skirt and boddice,
      And the sceptre of a whip ;—
    And the girl that drove the Reaper
      Drove the color from my lip.

I had compliments in plenty
  I could give, if I had time ;
But she swept them all as nothing,
  In confusion all sublime.
I could only gaze in silence,
  As she turned her team at will,—
And away the whirring Reaper
  Went beyond the swelling hill.

And I rode along unthinking,
  Save the vision I had seen,—
Of that little gipsy bonnet,
  And its fluttering bow of green ;—
And the riding-skirt and boddice,
  And the fresh young face I saw
Of the girl that drove the Reaper,
  On the fields of Pallidaw.

But once more I sought the Credit,
  And the sweet homes nestled there ;
And the girl that drove the Reaper
  Was as good as she was fair !
And I found the gipsy bonnet
  Shaded two enchanting eyes,
And her voice was set to music—
  But her heart was still the prize !

Can you doubt—the harvest over,
  And the sheaves all reaped and bound—
That my heart was bound among them,
  As if native to the ground !

And I bless the harvest-vision
   Of that little gipsy hat ;
And the girl that drove the Reaper
   Says, "There's two folks glad of that!"

CANADIAN WINTER SONG; 1884.

I sing you a Song of Canadian Winter :
   It is set to the tune of the jingling bells ;—
And its chorus hangs neither on speaker nor printer,
   But free in the bosom its melody swells.
Its step is the stride of the hardy snow-shoer,
   Its rhythm the sigh of the breeze through the pine,
And never Canadian suitor or wooer
   Cared more for his cause than I covet for mine!

We have built you, O brothers, a Castle of Brightness ;
   The stones were ne'er quarried, yet noble they rise !
Its turrets and Keep stand in beautiful whiteness,
   Its portals are open—it dreads no surprise !
O'er each icy turret the banners are streaming,
   Its panels emblazon St. Lawrence' clear wave,
And we walk or we glide 'mid the sparkling and gleaming
   Of diamonds as bright as Golconda e'er gave !

They wrong us who say that our Winters are dreary—
   That Happiness flies to some home in the South !—
Of our snow-lighted joys there are none of us weary,
   E'en Boreas blows *with a smile on his mouth !*

Then come to our Winter-sports! Come in your gladness,
    And bring with you kindness like that you shall meet,
And learn to retreat from the presence of sadness
    To Canada's Winter, and Ice-Palace sweet!

O come from the West, where the long grassy billows
    Are far as the sunset, and wide as the sea!
O come from the South, where the sick on their pillows
    Are dreaming of coolness, and gladness, and glee!
Come, buckle the snow-shoe, and mount the toboggan,
    Come, clamber the mountain, and shoot down its side;
And own, if you will, there's a long catalogue in—
    The sports of our Winter, and Carnival-tide!

The gleam of the Moon on each battlement lingers,
    And angle and arch scatter stars in a shower;
And the blushing Aurora with fair rosy fingers
    Is painting carnation on turret and tower.
The lights are all glancing in groups that are flitting
    Through hall and through portal, with laughter and
        song,—
And the fair icy Castle is royally sitting—
    The theme of the Bard, the delight of the throng.

You never saw Castle so dainty and daring,—
    Its walls so transparent, its turrets so bright;—
Nor yet does it lack, in its beautiful bearing,
    Within its broad halls, for fair Lady and Knight!
It rose as if fashioned by Fairy puissance,
    It flashes in sunlight, and towers 'mid the storm;
It never grows old in our sweet reminiscence—
    The Castle that warms us—*yet never was warm!*

We'll light up the life of the weak and the ailing,
    With the clear frosty air of our sunshiny days ;
The sleigh-bells and snow-shoes shall be more prevailing
    Than all the proud antidote Science conveys !
We'll bring back the bloom to the cheek that is faded,
    And send the new blood coursing warm through the
        veins ;
The heart that is saddened, the mind that is jaded,
    Shall find a relief where our Winter-time reigns !

When Summer, and sunshine, and gladness and glory
    Are flooding the earth, and the air, and the sea,
Our sources of happiness come like a Story
    To which we but *listen*, and laugh in our glee :—
But Winter *demands* we should make our enjoyment
    In converse and friendship with all, as we can ;
We are what we make ourselves ; Winter employment
    Is making acquaintance with mind and with man !

And, lovers and friends, I would rather your faces
    Were blooming in smiles for affection to see,
Than all the fine flowers with their colors and graces,
    That grow in the garden, or hang from the tree !
Then let the short Summer be lengthened out longer,
    And longer again, till it takes in the year ?
The sunshine of love in the heart growing stronger—
    The blossoms of kindness, that never grow sere !

Then out with the sleigh-robes, and rein up the horses !
    And let the snow batter from hoof and from heel !—
Command the toboggan, and vie with the forces
    Of Nature, in swiftness—no fear do we feel !

With snow-shoes, and sledges, and skates, and good
    nature,—
  A smile in the morning, a welcome at night,
We value our Winter, in every loved feature—
  The high noon of Friendship, the prime of Delight!

SONG: THE VIOLET.

I wandered through the garden,—
  'Twas the sunny time of flowers;
And the roving wind was wooing
  All the dewy morning hours.
There was fragrance in his breathing,
  As he rivalled bird and bee,
And whispered, gaily passing,—
  " They give all their vows to me !"

The marigold was flaunting
  With an eye and lip of scorn,—
While the peony was vaunting
  Of her queenly beauty worn.
And the sweet-pea says " Departing,"
  And the poppy says "Forget!"
But for the love I cherish
  I will wear the Violet!

I cannot clasp the queen-rose,
    For the thorns that may be there!
And I will not woo the jasmine
    With her prideful height in air;—
But I'll reach the violet hiding,—
    Even on my bended knee,
And wear it in my bosom,
    All for truest love to thee!

O, many flowers are blooming
    In the Summer morning air;—
To the light there's none so faithful,
    And there's none to me so fair!
Be it Summer, be it Autumn,
    Or in Spring among the dew—
I find the scented violet,
    With her eyes of faithful blue!

And though they smile upon me,
    Maidens by this saltless sea—
Yet amid them all I'm searching
    Still with longing eyes for thee!
But how poor, to heart so faithful,
    Must these weak comparings be!—
When next I seek for violets
    Let me bend the knee to thee!

SONG: THINK OF ME.

Thought is like a field of Summer,
    Where the flowers ungathered lie,
Waiting till some tardy comer,
    Led by beauty draweth nigh,—
And deems those best that humblest be—
Thus ever wilt thou think of me?

    Of me, of me, of me, of me!
    One glance, one look, one thought of me!

Not with such enrobing splendor
    As the sun's meridian tide,—
But with rays as sweetly tender
    As the moonbeam purified.
O let the mild reflection be
Of memory, when thou think'st of me!

Cho

Through the hours of vacant toiling
    Comes there many a thought of thee,
When the heart was near recoiling
    At ignoble destiny:—
One star above could light the sea,—
Thus star-like wilt thou think of me?

Cho:

Words are vain, when phrases perish,
    Vainly striving to express
What the inmost heart shall cherish,
    Sacred still, and fathomless !----
One wish may not too daring be -
All kindly wilt thou think of me ?

Cho :

Not as if each poor endeavour
    Sought some distant hopeless boon ;
Not as if our paths should sever
    Long ere hope should tell of noon ;—
But, for a thousand thoughts of thee,
Cast thou one trusting thought on me !

Cho :

SONG : THE MERRY MAPLE.

Hail to the merry maple,
    And the hills where the maple grows !—
The hills that hold no tryants,
    And the hills that fear no foes !
Where the green grain grows, and the sun fortells
    The harvest soon to be ;—
O, I would not give that Maple Land,
    For all the Lands I see !

Hail to the merry maple,
  And the feast and the fireside chair!
Where hearts were warm as embers,
  And the stranger welcomed there!
Where the white-winged waft of the feathery snow
  Made all seem bright within;—
O, I would not give that maple fire,
  For all cold Wealth could win!

Hail to the merry maple,
  And the Flag where the maple flies!
And still unstained and glorious,
  May it bless Canadian eyes!
And the march men make, with that flag above,
  Be such as heroes show;—
O, I would not give that Maple Flag,
  For all the flags I know!

SONG: THE VOLUNTEER OF '85.

TUNE: "DOUGLAS."

Lightly he left us, smiling, smiling,
  Soon to be back from the wars of the West;
Sadly he came amid weeping, weeping,—
  His country's flag wrapped around his breast.

I gave him a flower as he donned his helmet,
  He said he'd repay it with blossoms more dear;
But he never came back till in death cold sleeping,
  With prairie-flowers blooming upon his bier.

Kissing their hands to us, gaily they shouted,
   "We will do all that brave men can !"
Well was the promise redeemed, though to meet it
   The bravest died on Sascatchewan !

Envy me not for all that's left me—
   You have your heroes, and I have mine !
Yours come back with the thunder of cannon,
   And flags that are floating along their line :—

But I would not give mine in his youthful beauty,
   Sleeping the sleep of the brave and true,
Who lived for his love, and who died at his duty,
   For all the heroes that smile on you !

Sleep, soldier, sleep ! victorious though fallen :
   Dead to my eyes, to my heart yet alive !
Young, and so brave, and so bitter the parting—
   My Volunteer of the Eighty Five !

Scottish.

E'en then a wish, I mind its power,
A wish that to my latest hour
    Shall strongly heave my breast—
That I for puir auld Scotland's sake,
Some usefu' plan or buik could make,
    Or sing a sang at least!"

—Burns.

Scottish.

THE VALE OF TWEED.

WAS it some Bard, whose home was Earth's green sod,
All lands his country, and his father God,—
Who climbed the Border hills of mist and dew,
And told the World where Worth and Freedom grew?
Or, lured by love such maid could well inspire,
Albyn her home, a Scottish Chief her sire—
Adventurous youth from Roman campus freed,
First dipped his sandals in the fords of Tweed?
Crying, "But spare me on my wondering way,—
And wreck me, Fortune, as I backward stray!"*
Howe'er it were, or when, the world soon found
Beyond those hills, within that River's bound,
A Vale with pastoral beauty richly drest,—
A Land of gleaming lake and mountain crest,—
A People who amid the throes of war,
And darkly kneeling under baleful star,
Yet loved their land—each flower upon her breast—
And kept their troth, and made the stranger blest.

---

* Make me your wreck as I come back,
But spare me as I go!
              Old Ballad.

O vale of Beauty ! by each zephyr borne,
Still breathes the fragrance of that vernal morn ;
And every burn that babbles on its way
Prolongs the music of that earlier day !
Still beats the lark the thin resounding air—
Still in the den the hawthorn blossoms fair—
And o'er the moor, or on the breezy fell,
The maiden stoops to pluck the heather-bell.
O Scottish maiden with the sparkling eye !
Could'st thou be less than love and poesy ?
Or could the Bard that sues thee for a smile,
Cease from his ever-witching strains the while,—
Till, from the passion of one love-lorn swain,
The world, enriched, receives the deathless strain ?
Nor Grecian maid, with fillet round her hair,
With buskin'd feet, and brow and bosom bare,—
A fervid flower that blossoms in the sun—
Could e'er entrance the heart as thou hast done !
Still tread the moorland with thy flying feet,—
And in thy tresses bind the blue-bells sweet ;—
Still hold thy heart a prize for worth and grace,
Nor trust the semblance of a faithless face !
And long as wheels in space yon clouded sun—
While Spring returns, and haunted streamlets run,
Shall glowing Minstrel sing the Scottish maid,
And hearts beat time beneath the Scottish plaid !

Ye nameless Bards, who snatched the Scottish lyre,
And passing, swept the chords with patriot fire,
Till clarion blast returned the lyre unkeyed,
To drooping elm beside the rippling Tweed—

We stand beside each sacred mound, and say
"Some Bard, perchance, here waits a brighter day!"
And wonder, as we tune the sweet refrain,   [strain!
We all should know except the hand that waked the

O Land of Heroes! down this dewy vale
I hear the war-notes mingling with the gale;
And stubborn hosts with sturdy Border spear
And faithful claymore, from the shades appear.
Once more the battle closes fierce and far,
And Tweed's soft murmur dies in shouts of war.
Round Roxburgh's walls lie leaguring hosts again—
And Ancrum's moor is swept with sanguine rain.
From Ettrick's forest, archers, lithe of limb,
Twang the high notes of that keen battle-hymn;—
The peasant feels the hero in him stir;
As peals the cry of Douglas! Home! or Ker!
And ranks go down before the serried spear
Of dalesmen, charging home, with "JETHART'S HERE!"

The vision melts, the battle rolls away!
Through happy tears I see the lambkins play;
And lisping children throng the cottage door,
Where once the trampled heather blushed with gore.
The Martyr now may ply the patient spade—
A Hero's heart beat 'neath the Shepherd's plaid—
A Warrior's arm wide swing the peaceful scythe,
And martial Minstrel carol love-lays blithe.
All, all is calm; The Man is for the Hour;
The hour is peace; the sword is drawn no more!
Roll on, thou Tweed! in ripples to the sea,

And tell the waves thy dwellers all are free !
And this sweet peace, the dexter-chief of Life,
Is but the guerdon of our father's strife.
Scotland was plowed with anguish and with pain,
Watered with tears, and sown with precious grain :
And we are come—in Summer's ripeness come—
To reap, and keep, and sing the Harvest Home !

The men of peace outlive the men of war :—
These for a day—but those forever are !
The pilgrim sees those cairn-topped mountains rise,
But views them, Ettrick ! through thy Shepherd's eyes !
Nature with palpitating beauty rare,
We see, when Thomson kneels at shrine so fair :
Or when fair Science would our reason charm,
We tread her paths with Brewster arm in arm—
Look back, with Leyden, to lost childhood's meed—
Or sing the lays sweet Bonar hymned by Tweed !
And dream sometimes, as far the fancy flies
Through rifted clouds and undiscovered skies,
That HEAVEN is but another Vale of Tweed,
Without the memory of one shuddering deed—
Without its clouds, without its Autumn leaf,
Its fleeting gladness, or its following grief ;—
With purer sun, through blue and balmy air,
To tinge the mountains with a radiance fair ;—
And perfect men, to whom in love was given
To change the Vale of Tweed for Vale of Heaven !

THE NURSE O' MEN.

O, mony a ane can whistle
  That could never guide the plow;
And Souters may turn Sailors,
  That can neither steer nor rowe;—
And a man may bear a Scottish name,
  And dwell in Scottish glen,
Yet never hae the hero-heart
  That maks him king o' men!

I might hae been rich, my Jeanie,
  Gin I had lived for gold!
There was mony a ane to purchase,
  Gin I my heart had sold!
But I kent it lay wi' Scotland's sons
  To tak auld Scotland's part;
And her dear name, and thy sweet love
  Were life-beats in my heart!

Though whiles frae the pirn o' Sorrow
  Comes Love, the weft o' life,
Yet the sun will shine, my Jeanie,
  Through the mirky clouds sae rife!
And wha bides true to a' that's true
  Wins mair than gowden gear—
The balmy peace o' a heart at ease,—
  And hope and heaven sae near!

Fair gae they, and fair come they,
   That love auld Scotland weel !
Their waes gang in a forpit,
   Their guid come in a creel !
And aye the love that they may seek
   Be leal as that they gie,—
And in thy blessing, Nurse o' Men !
   Ilk son be bless'd wi' thee !

THE BORDER POET.

He was a man 'mong other men,
   Yet not the same as they—
But fashioned with a wiser ken
   From out the common clay.
The Laird is born to wealth and land,
   But his a nobler goal,—
For he was born by Teviot's strand,
   With music in his soul !

Where mountains green romantic swell,
   Where heath-flowers blush and bloom—.
The lonely glen—the breezy fell—
   The burn among the broom ;—
There, to the Poet seen and heard,
   The Muses swept along ;
And Nature in his bosom stirred
   The sacred fire of Song !

By ruined tower, serene and calm—
　　O'er fields where **Valor** trode—
By Martyr-graves, where, like a psalm,
　　The spirit soars to **God**—
There learned **he of the deathless past**,
　　To win a deathless name ;
As Scotland o'er the Poet cast
　　The mantle of her fame.

The Shepherd's cot his **Muses' cell**,
　　The **birds his** vernal choir,—
His Helicon was Wearie's Well,
　　And *peat* his Altar's **fire !**
No classic glories **thus were cast**
　　His childhood's **scenes among** ;
He made **them classic as** he passed,
　　And wove them in **his song** !

Of loves and lives of manly men,
　　And **charms** of blushing fair,—
Of worth that **hid in** lonely glen,
　　Of honor everywhere—
These were his themes in rustic grot,
　　The gloaming **to** beguile ;—
What though the World might hear him not ?
　　He lived in *Jeanie's* smile !

O gentle Bards from Border fells,
　　And Border **hills of** green !
For you what Scottish heart but **swells**,
　　Whatever seas **between** ?

We climb with you the lofty *law*—
 O'er flowery moorland speed,—
Or hear, beyond the birken shaw,
 The murmuring of the Tweed!

Sweet rest ye in your nameless graves,
 On near or distant shore?—
One burning tear your memory craves;
 Alas! we can no more—
But this, to keep sublime and pure,
 The love that tuned your lays
To Scotland's plaids, and Scotland's maids,
 And Scotland's lofty praise!

PEDEN'S PRAYER.

The Covenant is down, and a dastard wears the crown,
 And Scotland with a frown, bears her fetters as she
  may;—
And the sun looks down between auld Nithdale's hills
  of green,
 Where Cameron's grave is seen by the pilgrim on his
  way.

His was the rapid course of the torrent from its source,—
 The more we see its force, it the sooner meets the sea;—
For young his crown was won, and soon his race was run,
 And many a weary one with the Martyr fain would be!

And years had come and gane, since the day the martyrs
    slain
  (No more at Sanquhar's stane, but before The King on
    High!)
Had the COVENANT renewed, they had solemn sealed in
    blood,
  And in victors' robes had stood in the assembly of the
    sky.

And there amang the heather—his thin hands clasped
    together,
  And his weary glance up thither where the paths of
    victory lie—
And pleading for release, is Peden on his knees,
  And, "O to be wi' Ritchie!" is the burden of his cry.

The mountain-mist and snows had been sent to blind his
    foes,
  And when his cry uprose he was heard yet once again;
And the prayer his faith had spoken, received an answer-
    ing token,
  When the golden bowl was broken, and the Saint forgot
    his pain!

THE BAIRNIE.

When I left Scotland's shore, I took a bonnie bairn;
A toddlin' lauchin' thing, ower young her love to learn;—
I row't it in my plaidie, and pressed it to my heart,—
And aft the whisper 'tween us gaed, "We twa shall never
    part!"

The Simmer rose and fell ; the years gaed stalkin' by ;
And strength and vigor cam, and hope allured my eye ;
But the bairnie in my bosom is a bairnie ever syne,—
And what's the bairn's I canna tell, and what is only
    mine !

And aft the bairnie greets, at some auld ballad's wail,
And syne the bairnie smiles at the pawky Scottish tale ;
Till I can only say, " 'Tis the bairn, it is not I ;
For I hae dignity eneuch, were no the bairnie by !"

I've tried to hae it think and speak in foreign tongue,—
I've dune my vera utmost, and began the lesson young ;
But the bairn is just as Scottish as the day it crossed the
    sea !—
Ye tell me I should rule the bairn ! the bairn is ruling
    me !

I tell't it to my freend, and wad his wisdom learn,—
He said he was himsel just a muckle Scottish bairn !
And aye as I hae speir't, I find the glamour cast,
And the BAIRN WITHIN THE MAN aye is Scottish to the
    last !

O bairns that arena bairns ! whate'er the warld may say,
Aye cherish in your hearts the bloom that lasts for aye !
For he gangs blythest through the warld, and leaves maist
    guid behind,
Where Country, Love and Childhood are in his heart
    enshrined !

SONG: WEE JEANIE.

Jeanie's no the noble woman—
Wait the years that yet are comin',—
Jeanie's but a bairn, and human,
    Trippin' ower the lea;
Yet for een, the deepest, bluest—
Yet for heart, the sweetest, truest—
Graces maist, and fauts the fewest—
    First and fairest she!

If some Angel, downward pressing,
"Shook his wings," and breathed a blessing,
Thou has caught his sweet caressing,
    On lip, and brow, and ee :—
Gowd on every tress reposes—
Love's ane hue thy cheek discloses—
And like lintie 'mang the roses,
    Is thy voice to me.

Happy ye wha wins thy favor,
Blossom o' the mountain heather!
While the rolling years may gather
    Sober thought to me :—
But my youth, could I begin it,—
Love and life had I to win it,—
Life wi' my sweet Jeanie in it—
    Happy could I be!

THE BONNIE LAND.

" O weel ken I the Bonnie Land,
    Beside the Tweed it lies !
I ken the very nook o' the sky
,Neath which its pearls and gowans lie.
    And where its mountains rise !
Wi' Bimerside and Cowdenknowes,
Frae Newark Peel to the Loch o' the Lowes,—
Where laverocks sing, and heather grows,—
    O, that's the Bonnie Land !"

" O, that may be, and yet to me
    There lies my Bonnie Land !—
Where simmer streamlets glint and glide,
Through Carse o' Gowrie, fair and wide,
    And gray auld castles stand !
Where Tay, past mony a rock and scaur,
Flows saft as peace that follows war,
And Hieland hills look down from far—
    O, that's the Bonnie Land !"

" I ken, I ken the Bonnie Land—
    For I was cradled there !
'Tis not by Tweed, nor yet by Forth—
'Tis not on Tay, but in the North,
    Where beauty fills the air !
Where mountains beckon to the skies,
And locks are clear as maidens' eyes,
And glory on Glen Conan lies—
    O, that's the Bonnie Land !"

Up spak our wee wee gowdie-lane,
    The youngest o' them a',
"The Bonnie Land I weel can tell,
Is whaur my mither's gane to dwell,
    In yon sweet Far-Awa'!
The darksome night is never there,—
The morning light's aye rosy, fair,—
And weeping een can weep nae mair,
    Within that Bonnie Land!

"The weary heart shall win the balm
    That gars it sing for glee;
And saft as breath o' evening psalm,
The storm shall sink into the calm,
    Upon that simmer-sea!
And holy hearts shall harbor there,
Aneath the smile o' Angels fair;—
For He wha maks this warld His care,
    Maks THAT the Bonnie Land!

ROBERT FERGUSSON.

An incident strikingly illustrative of the unhappy destiny of the young poet, and at the same time of the honorable esteem in which he was held by those who knew him, **must not remain untold.** Shortly after his death a letter came from India directed to him, enclosing a draft for £100, and inviting him thither, where a lucrative situation was promised him. The letter and draft were from an old and attached school-fellow, a Mr. Burnet, whose name deserves to be forever linked with Fergusson's for this act of munificent, though fruitless, generosity. *Whitelaw's Book of Scottish Song: Introduction.*

"O come to the Indies, Rab!
    For the skies of the East are aglow;
There's hope for thy bosom, and light for thine eyes,
    There's wealth at thy bidding to flow!"
'Twas thus to the Minstrel he sent,
    With a pledge from his brotherly hand;
As he lay at noon in his sultry tent,
    And dreamed of his native land!

Swift sails the message bore
    Through spicy isles of the sea:
But the bard, or ever it reached the shore,
    Had laid down his head to dee!
They could kindle and glow at his strains,
    Or weep 'neath his minstrel wand,—
But they left him to die amid clanking chains,
    In the heart of his native land!

Alas, for a friend at hand,
    Wi' a bosom as tender and true—
And a cheering word for the hopeless bard,
    Like the lad ower the ocean blue!

Soon, soon was thy harp untuned
　　That might lang hae been strung wi' glee—
And mony wakened to find thee fled,
　　They wad hae gien gowd to see!

O sweetest and kindliest Rab!
　　Heart-broken, yet brither to a';
How young and how fair thy brow to bear
　　The sorrows that were thy fa'!
Like the MINSTREL wha set thee a stave,
　　The PLOWMAN LADDIE o' Ayr,
We'll drap a saut tear ower thy lowly bier,
　　And a' that lies buried there!*

OUR BONNIE BAIRN'S ASLEEP.

Our bonnie bairn's asleep;
　　And Angels constant keep
The jewel that's committit to their care;
　　And saft the smile we see
　　On lip, and brow, and ee,
A' silent now, and sightless evermair!

---

* The late true-hearted Scottish Poet, James Ballantine, took Fergusson's grave under his special care, and had a margin of shells round it brought from Ayr. After reading the above, he wrote to the author, "Should we have met when you were here, I should have joined you in your pilgrimage to Fergusson's grave, and shed tears together over the poor dear fellow and true Scotsman."

But when her een did close
In that lang rapt repose,
O think ye na they opened wide in light !
Light whaur the Saviour dwells,
Light whaur the music swells,
Through that lang day where never fa's night !

Far up, we trace her feet,
Alang the gowden street,
And waver her forrit, though our hearts are sair !
As near the awfu' Throne,
She fearless wanders on,
Conveyed by hands that ne'er kent human care.

O bonnie bairn, and blest !
Wi' heart and feet at rest !
Out ower thy path we'll hasten to our hame !
And He wha reigneth there
Will no despise our prayer,
For peace and pardon in thy Saviour's name !

SONG: THE PRISONER.

O she wha has my heart in thrall,
Is free on braes of Yarrow !
While I gaze on the vacant wall
That bounds my dungeon narrow.

The tyrant gives my sword to slaves,
　　My name to shame and sorrow;
But this brave heart he cannot buy
　　Is ever free on Yarrow!

I know the Spring is in the land,
　　The corn is greenly growing;
I feel the breath of Zephyrs bland
　　Upon my temples blowing.
I know her flowers are budding fair,
　　Afar from all this sorrow;
They bloom in Freedom's blessed air,
　　Upon the banks of Yarrow!

O softly breathe, ye fragrant winds,
　　Around that mansion olden;
And shine, thou son, with sweetest beams;
　　Make all her pathway golden!
And come, thou Hope, from 'mong the stars,
　　Speak of some blessed morrow,
When I shall burst these prison bars,
　　And rove with her on Yarrow!

SONG: LOCH SAINT MARY.

She was her mother's only child,
   On Yarrow braes a stranger lady,
And he was of the mountain wild,
   A shepherd in his hamely plaidie,
His soul looked out through poet's eyes,
And hers was heart beyond disguise,
And oft the sun looked in surprise
   Upon them by Saint Mary.

O sweet the lark on Yarrow braes,
   His widening flight of glory wringing;
But sweeter far that shepherd's lays,
   Read in the rapture of her singing!
Her clear blue eyes upon him bent,
Were ruin of his heart's content;
Nor wist she till the charm was spent—
   Two hearts lost by Saint Mary!

The only hand he e'er had kissed,
   Sae white and jewelled, would he dare it?
The only form his fancy missed
   In moorland cottage, would she share it?
Whate'er his fate, he'd dare it now,
And braye the worst with manly brow,
He vowed his love with many a vow,
   Beside the Loch Saint Mary.

She asked her **pride, and that said nay,**
    Some lord must wed the high-born lady ;
She asked her heart, and **that was aye**
    Still warming to the Shepherd's **plaidie** !
Now, never from yon summer skies
Falls light so sweet to lovers' eyes,
As round **that cot that nestling lies**
    Not far from **Loch Saint Mary** !

HABBIE SIMPSON.

O weel I wat the Hieland pipes
    Were never blawn **wi'** sic a birr,
At Wapinschaw by Tweed or Forth,
Or 'neath the star that's far'est North,
As when the soul of melody
Did, like **the swelling o' the sea,**
    Through Habbie Simpson stir !
But, like a cloud **that** darkly lowers,
A canker-weed in bed of flowers,
A hoodie-craw 'mang tappit hens,
A cawin' rook amang the wrens,
A jaggit thistle i' the sheaf,
A crawlin' oobit **on the** leaf—
Was the fell spark in Habbie's throat,
Not Corn Linn **could** e'er pit out !

He wakened frae a dreadfu' dream
O' lava-beds and crater-seam ;—
His vera banes were dried wi' heat,
His throat was like Pompeii's street ;—
"Janet!" But Janet couldna bring
Glenlivat frae the mossy spring :
And Hab, wi' grewsome face, and wae,
Drank a wee water, wersh and blae.
But Janet, lang afore the sun,
Had her eventful day begun :
And at the Laird's had made her mane,
For " Habbie Simpson, dead and gane !"
While Hab, at hame, had happed his head,
A sheeted corse—gin he were dead !

"Ay, ah," quo' Janet to the lady,
"I kenned, I kenned it wad come aye day !
But how to lay him in kirkyard,
   Is mair than I can tell or think ;—
For there's no a penny i' the house,
   Nor bite o' bread, nor sowp o' drink !"
The lady wad hae Janet ken,
She had her pity there and then ;
And when the laird cam in belyve—
He'd been our coursin' sin' 'twas five—
They wad consult about her case,
And baith befriend her in distress.
And then, weel-pleased, a basket filled
   Wi' bread and cheese, to show their pity :
Far better pleased was *she*, it held
   A bottle o' the *aqua-vitæ !*

The cheese and bread might weel be hained,
Till first the mountain-dew was drained!
Habbie grew unco blithe and gleg,
Wi' whiskey bizzin' ower his craig;—
Sae aft it gaed frae mouth to mouth,
It syne was dune, but no their drouth!
Then Habbie spak: " 'Twas rich and rare!
Noo, Janet, couldna' ye get some mair?"
"Na, na," quo' she, "it maun be *you*;
I've dune my turn; it's your turn noo!"

Hab wandered out by garden-wa',
And wondered whaur he'd gang ava?
He daurna' gang down to the laird's—
    They couldna' *twice* deceive the lady!
He couldna' gang to Lucky Caird's,
    An unco *score* was there already!
"Habbie!" It was the laird that spak,
Wi' twa three horsemen at his back.
"Ye'll come down to the Ha' the night,
And wi' strathspeys ye'll set us right;
Thir friends will hear the pipes wi' glee,—
For I hae *company* ye see!"
"Laird," quo' the piper, sad and wae,
"It wadna' look weel on this day,
Blawin' for gear, or blawin' for fame,—
My ain wife lyin' a *corp* at hame!"
"Is Janet dead?" "Ay, is she, laird!
And how to lay her in the yird,
    Is mair than I can tell or think;
For there's no a penny i' the house,

Nor meal to tempt a hungry mouse,
    Nor bite o' bread, nor sowp o' drink !"

"Weel, weel, my man, I'm unco wae
To think ye've faun on sic a day :
And canna thole a house sae bare—
Here a half-crown, till ye get mair !
And when I ance consult the lady,
To help distress ye'll find us ready."
The siller filled the bottle up—
The bottle filled the piper's cup :
Sae happy was he, fidgin' fain,
He scarce could let the pipes alane.
Till something he through window saw
That gar't him ding the cog awa !

But here the tale maun turn a wee,
And bear the laird sma' company.
The first word, loupin' frae his steed,
He heard, was " Habbie Simpson's dead !"
" Na, na, it's *Janet !*" quo' the laird,
" For *Hab* I saw by his kail-yard !"
" It's *Habbie !*" cried his lady gay,—
" Janet was here at break o' day,
And told us Hab lay dead at hame,
And' all the servants heard the same !"
" Hoot, toot, guid wife ! 'twas Hab himsel'
Ten minutes syne, tauld me his tale !"
" Now laird, ye're wrang ! 'twas Hab, I say !"
" 'Twas Janet !" " Habbie !" " Janet—pray
Let's say nae mair, my bonnie bird,

A woman aye has the last word—
But busk wi' bonnet, shawl, and gae
Wi' me to Habbie's on the brae,
And sure we'll a' be weel agreed
Wha o' them's leevin', and wha's dead!"

"Janet!" quo Habbie, "what way now?
The laird and lady's straught in view!
There's nae retreat in time of need!"
"Weel, weel! We'll just be baith o's *dead.*"
The laird saft chappit at the door;
An awfu' silence swept the floor!
Anither rap, then silent stands,
The open door still in his hands.
"Lang hae I ridden, far hae been,—
But o' sad sights that I hae seen,
A sadder ne'er before me spread—
A man and 's wife dead in ae bed!"
And then remembering the dispute,
Unsettled, wi' ilk witness mute,—
"I'd gie," cried he, "ten shillings free,
To ken wha first lay down to dee!"
"*Tin shillings*" struck on Habbie's ear—
'Twas twa three bottles mair o' cheer!
He sprang, and yerkit out his hand,
And roared like ane that had command,
"I'm drouthie, laird, wi' awfu' thirst—
Gie me the siller! *I* died first!"

How grief was gane, how mirth was seen,
How happy they were a' at e'en,

How Habbie's chanter loud did swell,
Whene'er the laird the tale wad tell,—
How Habbie charmed the guests aright,
Wha lang remembered that glad night—
Habbie was often heard remarkin',
To auld acquaintance at Kilbarchan.
But a' the country-side did say
That Hab and Janet, frae that day,
Kept frae the drink, and lived discreet ;
And a' men grat when Habbie dee't.

RAB MACQUHEEN AND HIS ELSHIN.

THE ARGUMENT. King Robert Bruce, gaun north, toward Perth, lilts a bit o' a sang some court poet had made about the Battle o' Bannockburn ; but I daur say it couldna' hae been muckle worth, for the rest o't has never come down till us. Comin' down by the Earn, and kennin' that Elspie MacQuheen had aye some guid kirn-milk, he behoved to be drouthie, and stoppit at her yett. She, waitin' on him, observed the heel o' his boot hinging lowse, and gar't her guidman, who was a Souter, yoke to, and gie't a steek. The auld tale is that the King wadna dism'unt, and Rab by a mischance ran his elshin *nine inches* intill the King's heel ! We may safely dispute the measurement, and no a 'thegither disbelieve the story—for I hae learned that traditions are mair apt to be true than to be lees ! If a' tales are true, the lang race of the MacQuheens o' the Brig o' Earn are now extinct—honest John McQueen, (Burns' "Souter Johnnie,") bein' the last o' them, whose banes lie peacefully in Alloway auld Kirk-yard ; (peace till his lingel!)

Our RAB aften promised Johnnie, na doubt, to sing the Sang o' Rab MacQuheen and his Elshin ; but Death faund him ower sune ! Doctor Currie was a' wrang, thinkin' Burns wantit to sing about Bruce and his grand deeds, in some lang poyem : it was his forgatherin' wi' Rab MacQuheen he was gaun to sing about ! Aih, me ! had he but leeved to do 't !

Dear Reader, haud yere breath, while, drappin' a tear, you and I, silently, DEDICATE THIS SANG—ettled, but never penned, by him that's now awa,

TO THE MEMORY O' BURNS!

" Hey for the Thistle ! Hey for the day
　　When the claymore swung i' the corn sae green !
When the Southron ranks were heaped like strae,
　　And we wan at the Bannock our kirn I ween !
Hey to the Thistle !"—Lost was the strain,
Ower the Ochills, and doun by the Earn,
As jingling doun by the shaw he's gane,
　　Bold King Robert, the gentle and stern.
Auld Fife at his back, wi' the Lowlands and Forth,
　　And the red, reeking field 'o that Midsummer day,—
Before him, the towering hills of the North,
　　And bonnie Saint Johnstoun, sweet upon Tay.
He looks to the right—the burn brattles alang,—
He looks to the left, the whins they grew strang ;
And gray and auld farrant, but peaceful and still,
Lies Rab MacQuheen's cot i' the bield o' the hill.

King Robert the dauntless was still but a man,
And a' men hae drouth sin' the warld first began—
The soldier bends down till he kisses the spring,—

For the Knight and the Squire the red wine they will
    bring ;—
Let the boor have his beer, and the herd have his whey—
The bairn its sowp milk at the close of the day,—
But come frae your wine, in your gowd and your silk—
The king of men ca's for a cog o' kirn-milk !

There's some love kirn-milk wha can never be great—
Poor wretches weel shaken by stepmother Fate !
But Kirn-milk and Greatness, like bees and red heather,
They're no easy sindered, the ane frae the ither !

Now Elspie MacQuheen, in her high-heeled shoon,
Tript down to the yett, a new mutch on her crown;—
" Wad his Highness light down ? wad his Highness come
    ben !
Or the lad tak his steed to the farm up the glen ?"
Na, he wadna light down, and he wadna come ben,
And his steed sudna gang to the town up the glen ;
" He'd reach Perth or Dunkeld—and the night wad tell
    whilk—
But e-now he'd hae nought but a cog o' kirn-milk !"
The milk it was cauld as the snaw on Macdhui,
As reamy and caller it cam till his mou ;   [round,
And he wiped his brown beard, and turned the bowl
And jingled his spurs, and looked on the ground,—
While Elspie was narrowly watching his heel,
'Neath the spurs o' red gowd, and greavlets o' steel.
" My Liege," cried the dame, " let Robin come out,
And pit a bit steek i' the heel o' your boot ;—
For I'm sure to hae't thus I never could thole,

Hinging lowse like the lip o' a mitherless foal!
Thae South-country Souters they never were better—
They're useless for shoon, but they're birkies for clatter!"
The time to dismount the King wadna spare,
And Rab and his elshin maun pit a steek *there*.
Rab cam, wi' his beld heid aye booin' and joukin',
And strack't 'gain the yett, for he wasna just lookin';
The lingel was strang, and the elshin was lang,
   The King was in haste, and hard the ben' leather,—
And Rab swat and reekit, and bored aye and steekit,
   Wi' the King and the dame lightly daffin' thegither.
Mischances come round just like the new moon—
Nae sooner we're up than we're sure to come down!
And Rab was just thinking he'd managed gey weel,
When awa gaed the elshin into the King's heel!
He loupit as though he wad never come down—
And, thinkin' a' wrang, his steed spun roun' and roun';
While Rab, a' dumfoundered to hae matters thus,
Had joukit and hid awa' 'neath a whin-buss.

"Rab, come here!" roared the King, "and tak out that
   elshin!
It's no on sic as thou a King's wrath sud he belchin';
But ken, my guid man, nane ever drew bluid
Frae Bruce i' the field, or Bruce i' the wood,—
In glen or on mountain, on seashore or sward,
But he found, or he ended, Bruce had the last word!
Sae here for the Souter that gars his King bluid,
I'll read thee thy riddle be 't evil or guid;—
Thy sons shall be Souters for twenty reigns lang,
And this fell steek o' thine be their hail fame and sang.

And yet the kirn-milk—rich, caller and free,
Demands, ane wad think, a wee token frae me;
And the King that rides North wi' a brod in his heel,
('To prove, like Achilles, he's no made o' steel!)
Wi' the flavor o' Ochill kirn-milk in his mouth, [South,
Like a breath frae the mountain, 'mang groves o' the
Says—'Elspie shall hae, as a token frae me,
The wee whinny knowe wi' the auld birken tree;
Wi' the cot and kail-yard for her and the bairn—
The cosiest beild on the banks o' the Earn!
And mind, ilka time a Monarch rides South,
Kirn-milk in a goblet ye'll hae for his drouth;
And an elshin and lingel present on a server,—
And ser' ye the King wi' the same zeal and fervor
Ye ser' your guid neebors wi' single-soled shoon;—
And lang be the hour or your sun shall gang down!"

The King rade; while Elspie was aff to prepare
A white linen bandage, sax ells lang, and mair;—
And Rab, stan'in' fair i' the sklent o' the sun,
Thought never his rays fell sae sweet on the grun',
As on that bit knowe wi' the whins blossomed ower,
And the green kail-yard at his ain sheiling door.
He was fu' o' land now! though ance hungry he'd been—
There's far mair nor Rab has than hunger, I ween!

Lang had the race o' the Souter been seen,—
Souters, a' Souters, frae Bruce to the Queen;
And doun frae Queen Mary to Jamie and Charlie,
Orange, and Hanover—hooly and fairly—
Souters, a' Souters, frae father to son—
Sock, buskin, jack-boot, and single-soled shoon.

How mony a day has ended in gloom,—
How mony a casket, when opened, is toom;
How mony a race wi' sturdy forbears,
Has dwindled and sunk in the whirlpool of years!
The Souter that drank wi' daft Tam o' Shanter,
   Johnnie McQueen, was the last o' his race;
And aft as our RAB, at the sound o' the chanter
   Hotched in his seat, as joy flashed ower his face—
Aye wad he promise some e'en when the Muse
   Cam for an hour, as the sheep sought the fauld,
RAB AND HIS ELSHIN they surely wad choose
   To sing for a sang o' the brave days o' auld!
But the Souter is gane, and RAB 's but a name
   That shines in the fore-front o' Scotland's best story;
And the sang now is sung wi' a faltering tongue,
   That might hae come till us wi' sparkles o' glory.

SONG: HAME AGAIN.

O gin I were hame again!
   As hame I wad be;
I'd part nae mair, for gowd or gear
   Frae my ain countrie!
For gowd is but the miser's hoard,
   And gear awa may flee;
But something better's to the fore,
   In my ain countrie!

O gin I were young again !
 As young I wad be ;
I'd live for love, and no for wealth,
 In my ain countrie !
For love will live when a' decays—
 'Mang snaw may blossom free ;
And weel I wat true love's at hame,
 In my ain countrie !

O gin I were blythe again !
 As blythe I wad be ;
My neebors should be happy a',
 In my ain countrie !
For ae blythe heart will comfort a'
 That round about him be';
And I hae found nae place for freends
 Like my ain countrie !

O gin I Teviot saw again !
 As Teviot I wad see ;
I'd ask there but a dreamless sleep,
 In my ain countrie !
For " hame is hame," whaure'er I rove,
 And that is hame to me !
O keep me aye a welcome smile
 In my ain countrie !

SONG: BONNIE ENEUCH.

Ye're bonnie, lassie; bonnie eneuch,
    To them that far in their favor set ye;—
And ower bonnie, far ower bonnie,
    To them that lo'e ye, and canna get ye!

O lassie, wae to Tam and me,
    That e'er we cam to the town o' Drassie!
But deeper wae I maun bear my lane,
    That ever I met wi' a scornfu' lassie!

I'm no sae young, and I'm no sae fine,—
    But I'm young eneuch to be broken-hearted;
I hae wared my love on a heartless quean,
    And youthfu' pride and joy's departed.

Ye're bonnie, lassie; bonnie eneuch,
    To them that far in their favor set ye;
But ower bonnie, far ower bonnie,
    To them that lo'e ye, and wad forget ye!

WALLACE WIGHT.

O Wallace wight! I see thee stand
   Before my fancy's ee,
The glory of thy mountain land,
   The hero of the free!
No braver arm, no keener sword
   Was e'er in Freedom's fight;
Nor gentler heart in lady's bower,
   Than thine, O Wallace wight!

Ay, let them rear, O Wallace wight,
   Their monuments to thee;
And crown the rugged Abbey Craig
   With emblems of the free!
And pilgrims from afar, survey,
   As sunward there they turn,
Where Wallace fought at Stirling Brig,
   And Bruce at Bannockburn!

But far beyond, O Wallace wight!
   All monumental art,
Thy name shall ever live in light
   Within each Scottish heart,
Thine arm alone upheld the strife,
   When hope itself was gone;—
When Albyn bled behind her shield,
   But still fought bravely on!

And but for thee, O Wallace wight!
  Had Freedom languished oft;
In every patriot heart, thy name
  Has borne his hopes aloft!
And thy claymore has raged, unseen,
  Through Freedom's darkest fight;
Till tyrant hearts have quailed before
  The shade of Wallace wight!

O Wallace wight! if e'er should be
  The foe within the land,
Then with a dauntless heart like thee
  Let Caledonians stand;
And, rolling back the invading tide,
  Hear Scotland proudly say,
" 'Twas thus they fought, 'twas thus they died
  For me, in Wallace' day!"

JAMES GUTHRIE.

1st June, 1661.

Ye men and breathren, hearken;
  Ye who have come to gaze,
And ye who oft have heard me
  Discourse of Zion's ways :—
I come this Summer morning,
  To lay this body down,—
I dare not seek its safety—
  I go to reach my crown!

I die not in my folly.
    For my faith is strong in Christ!
I go through weary wanderings,
    To keep an endless tryst!
I have preached his name to sinners,
    I have held his banner high, —
I have lived for Him and loved Him;
    And now for Him I die!

Had my life been evil-doing,
    I had not refused to die :
But I die because my Master
    Will not let me turn and fly.
To *these* I leave my blessing
    No more have I to give ;
To *those* my free forgiveness
    And pray their souls may live.

But oh, for thee, my country,
    My soul is sore distressed!
The land is full of swearers,
    Where once God's name was bless'd.
The Lord gave us deliverance,
    Yet we wear the yoke of sin ;
And set on high our idols
    His holy courts within.

Ye that with lamentations
    Do sigh and cry for sin,
Despair not of your Zion,
    For the Lord has joy therein!

A holy seed **shall** serve him,
    Though long the vision wait ;—
Hold fast your sacred Covenant,
    And **watch before his gate** !

And grieve not I should leave you ;
    My death shall **bring no stain** ;
I join **the blest Apostles,**
    And go with Saints to reign.
The Covenant live forever !
    Christ's Kingdom never **cease** !
Now, Oh my Blessed Father,
    Let me depart in peace !

THE MARTYR OF SOLWAY SANDS.

The tide was **flowing** on Solway Sands;
    And, bound to a rugged stake,
A fair-haired Scottish lassie stands,
    For Christ and Covenant sake.

She could die in **the bloom of her early youth**—
    (But **a** passing pang to die !)
But not one word of the saintly truth
    Could her guileless tongue deny !

The water had reached her praying lips,
    And dashed in her upturned eyes,—
And the swoon that led through Death's eclipse
    Was unfolding Paradise:—

But rough and torturing hands unbound
    The lass from the Martyr-stake:
And she found herself upon Scottish ground,
    Still mocked for Jesus' sake.

" Now swear to the King! or worse shall be!
    And abjure your *Covenant* vile!"
" Never!" she cried: " My King is He
    Who died for me erstwhile!

" I am His! I am His! I am bought with blood!
    Let me go where the Saints have gone!
I will pray for your King as I plead with God,
    But my troth's with Christ alone!"

And they bound her again to a rugged stake,
    In the hoarse advancing tide;
And they saw the gurgling bubbles wake,
    And the fair hair floating wide—

But they saw not the gleam of the white-winged host,
    Nor heard, as she heard, the strain
Of the ransomed ones on the Heavenly coast,
    Who answered the glad refrain,—

" Blessing, and honor, and glory and power,
 For ever and ever shall be
To Him who has saved us in Hell's dark hour,
 And made us His people, and free ! "

But the latest voice in that Heavenly lay—
 The clearest of all beside—
Was her's who went to her death that day
 In the Solway's flowing tide !

O Scottish Land ! at fair Freedom's birth,
 With what throes and pangs thou cried !—
It was not a loss, but a gain to Earth,
 That Margaret Wilson died !

ROBERT BRUCE.

7th June, 1329.

Came Summer in her smile of pride,—
 On every hill the light breeze sighing ;
But low at Cardross on the Clyde
 Lay Scotland's kingly warrior dying.

" My days have seen but stoure and strife,—
 I could not turn from Scotland's sorrow !
And the one dream I dreamed in life
 Has waited aye some flattering morrow.

"My sword, I vowed and vowed again,
　　From Paynim spears should slacken never,
　Until Jerusalem's sacred fane
　　Should stand emancipate forever!

"My soul, my vision's with my vow!
　　O Douglas, dost thou see them stricken?
　Go, seek the fight; my sword be thou:
　　And bear my HEART where dangers thicken!

"Drive the invader from the home
　　Of holy seer, and prophet weeping:
　Then lay my heart within the tomb
　　Where once my Lord in death lay sleeping!"

That sacred trust he onward bears—
　　Through distant lands still journeying ever;
　But fell amid the Moslem spears,
　　Beside the rushing Guadalquiver!

And when the fight was done, he lay,
　　With Bruce's heart, all foes defying!—
　In Melrose' ruined aisle to-day
　　The Douglas and the Heart are lying!

THOMAS THE RHYMER.

The Rhymer lay on Huntly bank ;
    While mystic memories drifted o'er him ;—
He raised his eyes at the armour's clank,
    And a steel-clad warrior stood before him.

" Now tell me, thou Rhymer ! " the warrior cried,
    " What is it that clouds thy brow with sorrow ? "
" The past was dark ! " the Seer replied,
    " But darker yet shall be Scotland's morrow !

" I see in vision his courser fall,—
    And Scotland's King lies crushed and dying !—*
I see, o'er Flodden's summit tall
    The shattered hosts of Scotland flying ! "

The warrior flushes—he holds his breath—
    On the pale seer his glance reposes ;—
" Now tell me, Rhymer ! on pain of death,
    What more thy mystic lore discloses ! "

" At Bannockburn can I see the Bruce
    The warlike pride of England shiver ;
And wring for us a blessed truce,
    Till Scotland's bleeding wounds recover.

---

* Alexander III.

"From Bruce's house shall they come to reign,
    From southmost sea to yon farthest Highlands;
And far and long shall sweep the main
    The blended Standard of the Islands!"

*   *   *   *

He kissed the Rhymer's quivering hand,
    And bowed with uncovered head before him ;
Then swiftly he sped adown the strand
    Yet still was the spell of that vision o'er him!

WALLACE'S FAREWELL TO MARION.

Farewell to thee, my Marion !
    For my sword must leave its sheath ;—
Mine arms are calmly folded,
    But the heart beats wild beneath !
I hear the distant thunder
    As the foe breaks on our shore ;—
Farewell to thee, my Marion !
    For I seek the field once more !

Farewell to thee, my Marion !
    We have parted thus before,
And kissed again in triumph
    As the foe fled from our shore :—

But now a boding whisper
   Says this shall be for aye ;-
Farewell to thee, my Marion ;
   For I seek the deadly fray !

Farewell to thee, my Marion !
   'Tis not in battle's hour
Thy warrior's heart shall fail him,
   Or his sword forget its power !
But who can wear a cuirass
   That is proof 'gainst treacherie ?—
Farewell to thee, my Marion !
   And farewell to libertie !

Farewell to thee, my Marion !
   They may wring thy faithful heart,
And dip their swords in Martyr-blood,—
   Thy faith shall ne'er depart !
But mine while life shall linger,
   And mine when death shall be !—
Farewell to thee, my Marion !
   My heart is aye with thee.

Farewell to thee, my Marion !
   The lore that lights my way
Foretells for bleeding Scotland
   A bright and glorious day !
And Wallace' blood shall moisten
   The soil where Freedom grows ;—
Farewell to thee, my Marion !
   And a welcome to my foes !

Farewell to thee, my Marion!
   I go from love and thee,
To strike for bonnie Scotland, —
   For her, for her to dee!
My name, and fame, and honor,
   I leave with her for aye ;—
Farewell to thee, my Marion!
   And farewell the light of day!

BURNS.

FOR A SCOTTISH GATHERING.

Like as a Scottish sodger thinks,
   Whatever else betide him—
On foreign shore—by Stirling's Links—
   That WALLACE stands beside him!
Sae wheresoe'er our lot be cast,
   By wood or winding river,
The spirit of the mighty Past
   Is o'er our souls forever!

And in that vision o' langsyne
   What rapture is, and glory—
Where ROBIN trills the tuneful line,
   And guides the touching story!

We see his artless Bonnie Jean,
    Or Tam, wi' witch and **fairy**,—
And weep to think *what might have been*
    For Burns and Highland Mary!

We trod the hills with firmer step,
    That Burns had trod before us;
And dreamed each feathered warbler kept
    Some Caledonian chorus!
Or furrow drew wi' tentie care,
    Though less it needed guiding—
The Minstrel frae the banks o' Ayr
    Was by the plowman striding!

Aih, Sirs! could Robin been advised
    To life's amended issue!
A *new edition,* read, **revised**,
    Correct in every tissue!
But they who might his mentors been,
    Were tempters all beside him;
They tippled wi' him morn and e'en,
    But never sought to guide him!

I tell you, friends! we'll look nae mair
    At ilk lamented failing—
But like the laverock high in air
    Beside some cloudlet sailing,
We hae his thoughts, his words, his sang,
    Like some sweet story olden,
To fire us as we plod alang
    Toward our sunset golden!

If Independence in the heart
    Has ever won its measure—
If loves and lives of manly men
    Have given the world a treasure
If on the brow of honest Worth
    A halo e'er has lighted,
Thank Burns! who taught that nevermore
    Should man by man be slighted!

To us, in cabins of the West,
    Or some young city viewing,
With Scottish lore Burns gives a zest
    To all that's worth pursuing!
We stand, with him, for God-given right
    Of life, and love, and labor!
And every man's a Scot to-night,
    And every Scot "OUR NEIGHBOR!"

OUR HAME IS WHAUR WE MAK OUR NEST.

Our hame is whaur we mak our nest,
    By wood, or wave, or winding river;—
Our bed is whaur we gang to rest,
    To dream o' happy days forever!
And as the bride, some dear burnside
    Forsakes, to follow love's sweet tether,

And maks her hame o' joy and pride
    Whaure'er her treasures draw thegither,—
Sae we, ayont the saut-sea faem,
In dear Canadia find our hame!

We hae na changed our scorn o' pride,
    Our love o' right, and worth and honor,—
Nor left by Tweed, or Tay, or Clyde,
    What Scotia's noblest sons have won her!
But aye the same in Western hame,
    As 'neath her skies, or 'mang her heather;
Kent aiblins by anither name,
    As round her ingleside we gather, —
Canadian ilka branch and shoot—
The stock some sturdy Scottish root!

O weel I wat, we'll gie her praise—
    Our ain Dominion, calmly lying;
Where Freedom's wing has fanned her braes,
    And love on ilka breath is sighing!
How hae we smiled to tame the wild,—
    Through virgin soil to steer the furrow, —
Or how the house-logs high we piled,
    To bield us frae some wintry morrow!
Yet underneath that humble shade
How sweet the hame that love has made.

Frae billowed lakes that glint afar,—
    To Northern mountains grandly swelling,
That lean against the Polar s'ar,
    And keep the postern o' our dwelling;

Sic braid domain! sic fields to gain,
　　Unfought by sword, by share unfurrowed!
Sic tales to tell o' hill and plain,
　　Or sing in native strains unborrowed!
Nae minstrel harp can e'er be tame
That fitly sings our Norland hame!

As when the frugal meal is ower—
　　Ilk want supplied, and care discarded,
We own the sweet enchanting power
　　O' strains till then a' disregarded;
Sae hae we here, for mony a year,
　　Been sae intent wi' field and *fallow*,
The Muse's voice we scarce could hear,
　　By fount, or flood, or hazel-hollow!
Our bread is won, the fight is ower—
Canadia's Muse, we own thy power!

We'll sing, with thee, the lochs and springs,
　　The woods and wilds, by hill and river,—
The cloudless skies—the thousand things
　　That mak our hame a joy forever!
Frae Breton's tide to Huron's side,
　　How mony happy hearts replying,
Wi' a' a nation's new-born pride,
　　Thy lofty mien and glance descrying—
Ca' thee to sing sae loud and clear,
That a' the listening warld may hear!

Sweet hame o' joys that yet may be;—
　　In bygane days our pride and glory;

Wi' bosoms leal we turn to thee,
   And read our record in thy story !
In war or peace, a hardy race,
   Aye free in spirit, thought, opinion—
Shall, rising, fill their fathers' place,
   And love, as we, our ain Dominion.
Wi' love that flows like Lawrence' flood,
And deep and boundless as thy wood.

Oh ! ither lands their gowd may sen',
   And spicy forests there may flourish ;—
Canadia, thou that rearest *men*,
   A nobler *crap* that theirs can nourish !
Thy maids as fair as forms o' air
   That flit amang our dreams beguiling,—
Wi' peace in ilka prospect rare,
   And plenty ower the landscape smiling ;—
Fu' fain we linger ower thy name,
And bless our dear Canadian hame !

CRAWS.

TO MY FATHER,

WHASE LOVE TO SCOTLAND, AND HER VERA CRAWS,
IS AS PURE AS HIS AIN SNAW-WHITE POW,

THIS POEM,

WHICH RECOUNTS SOME O' HIS AIN EARLIEST HISTORY,

IS DEDICATED.

It is na every man that kens a *craw*!
This I lay down as universal law;—
For weel I wat a craw's like ither folk,
And keeps his mind weel hidden in a pock.
Wha kens a craw, was *bred* amang the craws!

Kent them afore the horn-book or the tawse,—
Thought their rough speech a dialect o' his ain—
Kent when they prophesied o' cauld or rain;—
And never lookit to the lift on high,
But saw a *craw* between him and the sky!

In days langsyne, auld Scotia's pennon flew,
At some spear-heid, a simple streak o' blue,—
Till chiels would hae the *Lion* standard rear't,
And spak o' *dexter, azure, gules* and *vert*.
" Na, na," said Sandy o' the Knowe, at Scoon,
When auld King Kenneth first pat on his crown:
" Nane o' your *lions*, roarin', rampin' through,
Tearin' and slayin' till his wame is fu';

But gin ye want an emblem fit and braw,
Tak my advice, an' let it be a *craw* !
He's a' our ain, like thrissle-taps an' heather,
And far mair like a Scotsman a' thegither ;
Sae cannie, slee an' pawkie to the sight,
An' circling lang roun' whaur he means to light ;
Wha keeps frae girns and snares like you and me,—
And, saw wha will, *his* corn is growin' aye !".

Ah, Sandy, man ! but weel ye kent the mind
O' craws, and lions, and the human kind ;—
I doubtna', in auld books judicious walin',
But ye'd be foun' the Patron Saint of Crailing !
Sweet Crailing ! wi' thy streams, and haughs and woods
As fair as e'er were found aneath the cl'uds ;
How sweet to watch the spring come like a blush,
Ower maiden's cheek, on ilka tree and bush,
When laddies ran to allure the ascending trouts,
And, mad wi' joy, brak out in hoys and shouts !
The vera Teviot, rowin' through the haughs,
Now brattlin' on, now gliding 'neath the saughs,
Partakes the influence o' sweet Nature's laws,
An' sings in unison wi' Crailing's craws !

Many a' the howffs o' craws, frae Banff to Cheviot,
There's nane like Crailing i' the haughs o' Teviot ;—
Sic grand assemblies i' the upper air,
Circling in solemn state, in hunders there ;
Some statesman-project surely there was born,
Nor ane wad condescend to think o' *corn* ;
Yet ne'er a field was sawn, the parish through,

But 'twas discussed frae every point o' view ;
The plot was cleckit i' the sunset-blaze—
The field was harried or the plowman raise !

But when cam Martinmas, and then cam Yule,
And winter's wine was seen in ilka pool,—
When trees were bare, and stibble fields were white,
An' a' the insect tribe were out o' sight,—
How humble were the craws ; how honest, pure,
As shiverin' roun' the trees frae hour to hour,
They tauld o' auld misdeeds in field and tree,
And vowed strang vows o' honest poverty.
(There's naething like a hungry wame, to gie
A strength to humble, virtuous honesty !)
Ane wad wi' waefu' voice his neebor tell
What to a Cottar he had dune himsel',
Howkin' his wee bit crap out o' the grun',—
Till sune the man was roupit out an' dune !
Ithers confessed, in penitent narration,
How they had held a three-days' jubilation
'Mang mattent stooks, wi' sair an' bursten wame,
An' a' the wyte was laid upon the *game*.
Anither humbly owned the desecration,
How, near Lord Cranstoun's vault he took his station,
And when the beadle till his kail had gane,
He in, and whuppit aff a dead man's bane !
Till ane wad think the craws wad steal nae mair,—
Just nip a worm ahint the plowman's share,—
Or i' the woods, amang the leaves an' faggots,
Wad honest scart for speiders, bugs and maggots.

But ah, how dim an' low repentance burns,
When tempting opportunity returns!
Ower sin unseen we easy victories gain,—
The sin, returning, brands us for its ain!

Cauld Candlemas had passed, when auld wives said
The first stick o' her nest ilk craw had laid;
An' early Spring cam in wi' flowery feet,
An' scattered cowslips wide, and daisies sweet,
Wee birds cam back frae lands ayont the seas—
The bleat o' lambs was borne upon the breeze—
And farmers early out to pleugh and saw,
Gained great applause frae every honest craw.
I canna tell, whether in Crailing craws
Memories were short, or what might be the cause,
But weel I ken, when genial Spring cam in,
Ilk thievin' craw fell until his auld sin!

The Minister, guid man, wha humm'd and hae'd,
In parish Kirk, a quiet honest trade—
Wad pleugh his glebe, and hae it sawn wi' corn;
An' down the haugh wi' active feet was borne
In search o' some bit callant, wha might herd
The new-sawn field, and save the tender braird.
Now Jockie was a wee and active laddie,
Could play fit-ba' as weel as onybody—
Catch minnons, set a girn, or clim' a tree—
An' as for duds—weel, let the laddie be!
Duly installed, behold him at the Manse;
Now let the craws and him just tak their chance!

A week had passed, and Jockie to the Schule
Gangs marchin' in, according to the rule ;
Lang, dark, severe, the Dominie sternly raise—
" Where have you been, sir, for these several days ?
Confess your truantry !"   The laddie stared
First at the Dominie, and then at tawse upreared,
" I was herdin' "—then he lookit at the tawse—
" I was herdin', herdin', Sir—*the Minister's craws !*"
The parson, when he heard the kind o' flock
He thus was said to keep by little Jock,
Drew out his snuff-box, made a cautious wale,
And hotched and leuch at the wee laddie's tale ;
" Deed, laddie, mony a ane like me avows,
His flock is unco mair like *craws* than *dows !*"

Wee Hughie gied awa up Te'iot side,
For service at some lane farm-house to bide,
He missed the murmur o' sweet Owsenam Water,
He missed the cheery road wi' ceaseless clatter ;
He missed the aiks, the lime trees, and the haws,
He missed the vera music o' the *craws !*
His heart was sick, he couldna eat his bread—
'Twas hame, 'twas hame, was ever in his heid !
The only thing that gied a blink o' joy,
Was whiles a hame-like craw came sailin' by.
He kent they a' had left some Crailing tree,
And grat to hae the wings a craw could gie !
Wi' wistfu' een he watched ane sailin' by—
His heart gaed out in ae despairin' cry,
As down his cheeks the bitter tears were hailin',
" Aih craw ! craw ! When saw ye *Crailing ?*"

Aye, mony a ane like he's been sick for hame,
And dee't for something that they couldna name !
For who sae loves auld Scotland's vera craws,
Loves Scotland's sel', her scenes, her folk, her laws ;
And to the utmost screed o' earth conveys
His country's worth, her valor and her praise !

There's some wad live wi' rhetoric and wi' grammar,
Ithers by knappin rocks wi' a wee hammer ;
An' some wi' *Lingua Franca* sputtering jargon—
Whether they're man or ape it's just a bargain !
But tak a Scotsman frae his border hills,
Where loud and far the whistlin' plover wheels,
Let him but tread the moss o' Ancrum Moor,
And learn tradition's patriotic lore,—
Gie him his spells, his carritch, A. B. C.
An' mathematics to the Rule o' Three ;—
He'll get his grammar frae the friendly craws,
He'll learn philosophy frae Nature's laws—
Philanthropy is but his heart's ain power,
And love but Jeanie's glance at gloamin's hour !
Thus gaed they out frae burn, and haugh, and plain,
Whase power and eloquence were a' their ain ;
Wha little owed to schules, or buiks, or lear,
Owed something aiblins to the craws in air,
To Science less—an' to rough sense the mair ;
Yet nicked their names on tally-stick o' Time,
And made auld Scotland and themselves sublime !

Where Jedworth's Abbey rears its heid aboon,
An' daws and swallows sweep wi' endless roun',

Where lady-tourists stick in winding stair,
An' mair ye seek, ye'll aye find out the mair,
Where DAVIE BREWSTER sought scholastic study,
As lang syne JAMIE THAMSON on a cuddie ;—
Where sweeps the wind through learning's chosen nooks
An' cloisters nae mair even *smell* o' books—
There still, wi' curious een the stranger sees,
Aboon his heid, and 'mang the traceries
An' supple carvings o' the storied stone,
The sturdy monograms o' Abbot John
"𝔍𝔬𝔫 𝔍𝔞𝔩," ye read aboon the springing arch,—
"John Hall? and wha was he?" ye fain wad search,
Up Owsenam Water ye may whiles discern
On wee bit knowes, a something like a cairn ;
Just a green heap where some auld lum was foun',
That lang survived the crumblin' wa's aroun' ;—
In siccan cot stout Abbot John was born,
A rowlie-powlie callant, a' forlorn.

He owned nae teacher but the Crailing craws—
He scorned a' schules, and books, an' sclates, an' tawse,
Aye rammin' information down his throat
By "Rule o' thoomb," without a book or note ;—
He sune faund Crailing haugh ower sma' a "sphere!"
An' hint King David marched wi' sturdy spear.
An' when the King wad big a stately pile,
To be a light amang the Sons o' Toil,
To lead the Borderers in Learning's ways,
An' tune their *slogans* into psalms o' praise,
Wha to his aid might he sae fitting call,
As honest, upright, downright, douce John Hall ?

An' when, admiring, ye wad learn the cause,
Mark, 'twas the *craws* that made him what he was!

Sae to our sage conclusion straught we come—
Wha learns to speak frae *craws*, will ne'er be dumb!
Wha learns his *grammar* frae their voice in air,
Will aye be ca'd " a nat'ral *orator;* "
Wha learns the wisdom o' their council-trees—
His heid to carry wi' sic courtly ease—
To keep as free as they frae traps an' girns—
An' wind as few o' dark misfortune's pirns,—
Wha has as mony frien's o' his ain kind,
An' leaves as few untasted joys behind!—
Wha keeps as weel his color to the last—
(" Wash a craw *white!* " no Parliament e'er passed!)
An' keeps as ready for the next guid chance
As the glib craw, wi' his slee pawkie glance,—
Will mak a guid, fair, average, cannie Scot,—
Determined to be happy wi' his lot :—
Scotland aye *first*, her honor and her cause,
Her bards, her mountains—nay, her vera *craws!*
Himsel', in modest place aneath her ee,
For weel he kens she is, *whate'er her sons shall be!*

Note.—Crailing is an ancient hamlet, at the junction of the Oxnam Water with the River Teviot; on the opposite side of the Teviot from the battle field of Ancrum Moor. It is two miles from Jedburgh. The Dominie was Robert Aitken, father of the late celebrated Revivalist, Rev. Robert Aitken; and grandfather of the noted English Evangelist, Rev. Hay Aitken. Jedburgh Abbey is a fine old ruin. It was founded by David I. The cloister is still shown, where, in modern times, a Grammar School was kept, at which Thomson of " *The Seasons,*' and Sir David Brewster were educated. Of "Hughie" I know nothing more than I have told. The occurrence was real, as was also that of my father, "herding the Minister's craws!" I am not aware that Abbot John's history is known, but I thought it a pity so enterprising a man should have none, and so I gave him one. Crailing was the ancient seat of the Cranstouns.

SONG: THE HIGHLAND LADDIE.

O the bonnie Highland laddie!
    On his hills beside the sea;—
Wi' his cheek sae fair and ruddy,
    And the love-light in his ee :—
There are smiles and beauty waiting
    In the happy days to be ;—
O the bonnie Highland laddie!
    There is light and love for thee!

O the honest Highland laddie!
    In his shieling by the burn,
Wha can wear his humble tartan,
    But a crown dishonored spurn.
O the world has wealth and honor
    For the true and for the tried ;
O the honest Highland laddie!
    Be thine honor a' thy pride!

O the merrie Highland laddie!
    Wantin' sorrow, wantin' shoon ;
Chasing laverocks 'mang the heather,
    Puffin' cheeks out like the moon :—
They are saut tears for the shedding,—
    May that flow be ne'er thine ain!
O the merry Highland laddie!
    Seek nae grief, and feel nae pain!

O the gallant Highland laddie!
    Wi' an arm to guard the right;—
And a brow that burns and flushes
    With a conscious inner might.
There are wrangs that maun be righted,
    There are triumphs yet to be;—
O the gallant Highland laddie!
    There is glory waits for thee!

Wha could meet thee, Highland laddie,
    And his heart no be thine ain?
True and gentle, leal and ready,
    Prizing honor mair than gain:—
Evil lifts its head around us,
    Scotland's ills are sair to dree;—
But we trust thee, Highland laddie,
    Wrang shall never bear the gree!

SONG: WI' THE LAVEROCK I' THE LIFT.

Wi' the laverock i' the lift, piping music i' the skies,
When the shepherd lea's his cot, and the dew on gowan
    lies—
Up, up, let me awa frae the dreams the night has seen,
And ask what is the matter wi' my heart sin' yestere'en?

The laverock i' the lift, i' the wildest o' his flight,
Sees whaur his love abides, wi' throbbings o' delight,—

But I behold her cot, and awaken to my pain—
It canna sure be love, or I'd sune be weel again !

Adown the sunny glade, there's a bower that cottage nigh,
Whaur the flowers aye are sweetest, and the burn gangs
    singin' by,—
'Twas there we partit late, wi' a kiss or twa between,—
But what can be the matter wi' my heart sin' yestere'en?

I'll to yon garden hie, ere the gloaming close its ee,
I'll tell her o' my pain, and ask what it can be?
It may be she can cure wha gar't me first compleen,
For aih ! there's something wrang wi' my heart sin'
    yestere'en !

SONG: BESSIE BELL AND MARY GRAY.

Frae bonnie Saint Johnstoun he hied on his way,
To seek Bessie Bell, and to seek Mary Gray ;
For doun by the burn they had biggit their bower,
And wi' lang simmer rashes they theekit it ower.
And wi' lang simmer rashes they theekit it ower..

There were nae twa lasses sae fair and sae free,
'Tween the blue Hieland hills and the sough o' the sea ;
And blythe were the threesome that lang simmer day,—
For they baith loved the lad, and he loved Mary Gray.
For they baith loved the lad, and he loved Mary Gray.

But the plague it was sair, and the land it was wae,
There was sighing and sabbing by night and by day ;—
And e'en to the bower where the lassies had gane,
The spoiler cam down, as he numbered his ain !
The spoiler cam down as he numbered his ain !

The sun, or he set, keekit under the theek—
Nae smiles now o' welcome, nae voices to speak ;
And mony a heart at the tidings was wae,
For sweet Bessie Bell, and for sweet Mary Gray.
For sweet Bessie Bell, and for sweet Mary Gray.

For Bessie was fair as a floweret in dew,—
Her smile was sae sweet and her een were sae blue ;
And Mary was blythe as a morning in May,—
They baith loved the lad, and he loved Mary Gray.
They baith loved the lad, and he loved Mary Gray.

Their kin lay in Methven, wi' statue and urn ;—
But they wad lie under the mools by the burn ;
They wad sleep na in Methven amang their proud kin,
But laigh 'mang the breckans, to beek i' the sun !
But laigh 'mang the breckans, to beek i' the sun !

SONG: THE BROOM OF THE COWDEN-KNOWES.

NEW SET.

O take away this silken robe,
    Put off this gaudy plume ;
And bring to me the simple snood
    I wore amang the broom !
O the broom, the bonnie, bonnie broom,
    The broom of the Cowdenknowes ;
I wish I were at hame again,
    Herding my father's yowes !

My life was like the birdie's flight,
    In Simmer's sunny air ;
As little heeding of the night,
    As unacquaint wi' care.
O the broom, the bonnie, bonnie broom,
    The broom of the Cowdenknowes ;
O let me dream o' hame again,
    And the milking o' the yowes !

O flowers are sweet for the joys they gie,
    And no for the name they bear ;
And I wadna gie the bonnie broom
    For the flowers o' a' the year !
O the broom, the bonnie, bonnie broom,
    And the lassie wi' her yowes !
The vera warld seemed lapped in gowd,
    I' the broom of the Cowdenknowes !

'Twas 'mang the broom I lost my heart—
　　Ane lo'ed me lang and weel;
How could I turn my back on Tweed,
　　And break a heart sae leal?
O the broom, the bonnie, bonnie broom,
　　The broom of the Cowdenknowes;
And the vows we made betwixt us there,
　　At the faulding o' the yowes!

I've seen how vain is pride and state,—
　　How light are lordling's vows;
And I'll e'en away to the heart I brak,
　　And the broom of the Cowdenknowes.
O the broom, the bonnie, bonnie broom,
　　The broom of the Cowdenknowes;
I wish I were at hame again,
　　Herding my father's yowes!

SONG: FARE THEE WEEL!

Fare thee weel, bright Land of Story!
Scottish glens, and Scottish glory!
Battle-strath, and haunted river—
Bright in memory's page forever!

Fare thee weel, ilk mountain sheeling!
Beauty rare and worth concealing;—
Human love in blossoms tender,
Mixed with Nature in her splendor!

Fare thee weel, thou Lowland maiden!
Ken'dst thou how my heart is laden,
E'en thy scorn to-day, might borrow
Ae sweet glance of love to-morrow!

Fare ye weel, ye scenes of pleasure!
Love and hope in wasted measure;—
Far I flee o'er Western billow,
Sunset lands to make my pillow!

Fare ye weel, ye flowers that blossom
Spring's tiar, and Summer's bosom!
In the shaw, and 'mang the heather,
Grace and sweetness linked thegither!

Fare thee weel, ilk warbler's story!
Laverock at the gates of glory,—
Purling streams that sing forever—
Highland loch, and pebbled river!

Fare thee weel, bright Land of Story!
Still thy name shall be my glory!
'Tis thy love to me imparted,
Gars me gae sae broken-hearted!

SONG: WILL YE TAK ME?

"Will ye tak me?" she cried, as the night cam on;
"Will ye tak me?" she cried, wi' a weary tone;
  And the braw young laird o' Harriston Ha'
  Lookt down as he passed, at the garden wa'.

And he saw nocht there by the garden wa',
But a lintwhite heid, and a breist o' snaw;
And a wee bit dud sark o' Paisley yarn,
And the wee bare feet o' the mitherless bairn.

And he turned awa, as he proudly sat—
"Let ithers tak in the beggar's brat!"
And he passed awa wi' a loud guffaw,
To join in the revels of Harriston Ha'.

Yet faund she friends, and hame, and bread;
And a Kind Hand lifted her drooping heid;—
And the mitherless bairn grew wondrous fair,
As the lintwhite heid turned gowden hair:—

And the love-light shone in her een sae fair;
And her sweet soul stood at the windows there;—
And the laird now wad gane for mony a mile
But to catch ae glance, or to win ae smile!

But she gaed her heart to ane that was true,—
Hand, gowd, beauty, and een sae blue;—
The laird wadna tak her when greetin' her lane,
And she wadna tak *him*, when he was fain!

SONG: THE GAY GOSS-HAWK.

"O come to me, thou gay goss hawk,
    That baith can speak and flee,—
And hie thee to my lady-love.
    And tell me how is she?
Ye'll ken her by that beauty rare
    The warld ne'er saw before—
Ye'll ken her by the birk sae fair
    That blooms fornent her door."

O ance again, thou gay goss-hawk,
    Come near, and speak to me,—
And show me what my true love said,
    And what she sent by thee.
"She sent thee here a gowden ring,
    A garland o' her hair—
And at Saint Mary's Kirk on Tweed
    She bids thee meet her there:"

O pale, pale now that lady grew,
    And dim her sunny ee;
"O father, dear, a dying wish
    I pray thee grant to me!
Though thou didst scorn my Scottish love—
    His banishment decreed—
Yet lay me in Saint Mary's Kirk'
    Beside the murmuring Tweed!"

O sadly now approached the bier,
  And loud the weeping grew ;
Her lover there, with mony a spear,
  Asked he the corse might view.
The deadly draught had wrought its spell,—
  The lady oped her een !
And Scotland won the fairest bride
  That England e'er had seen !

SONG: LOUIE CAMPBELL.

The purple mist hangs on the brow of Ben Cruachan,
  And sparkles at morn in the dews of the vale ;
But purer and brighter is she of Balmoral,
  That chooses her lot in the Land of the Gael !
There are Campbells in council, and Campbells in battle,
  And Campbells as fair and as bright as the morn,—
But the fairest and brightest that e'er wore the tartan,
  Is sweet Louie Campbell, the Lady of Lorn !

Let the sun shine in beauty on high Bedan-amran,
  And waters in music descend from Loch Awe ;
The winds be a pibroch of triumph and glory,
  To hail the best day that the Highlands e'er saw !
She has left her proud home in the old royal towers,—
  And the side of the throne, in whose shade she was born,
And wrapt her within the green plaid of the Highlands,
  The sweet Louie Campbell, the Lady of Lorn !

No more shall the Gael, on her own Loch Etive,
  Look sadly away to a grave o'er the deep;
But nourished at home, like his own Mountain-heather,
  Take root in the soil where his forefathers sleep.
No more shall the moorcock and grouse take the place
  Of the cot of the Clansman sublime in his scorn;
But gentle and brave, in the shade of his mountains,
  He'll bless Louie Campbell, the Lady of Lorn!

There's glory to win in the wide world before him,
  And fame to the Clansman is calling afar;
But gladly he'd leave all his fame and his glory,
  To please the blue eyes of the Lass from Braemar!
Who thinks that the Highlander e'er is unfaithful,
  Or the love of the Gael not a gem to be worn—
Let him go where the sceptic is silenced forever,
  And ask Louie Campbell, the Lady of Lorn!

SONG: BRING A WHEEN LAVEROCKS!

The lark has been successfully introduced into Southern Ohio; and doubtless would live and sing in Canada—to the unspeakable delight of thousands of Scottish hearts and eyes.

  The wind-flower wakens from winter's sleep,
    On the verge of the vanishing snow;
  And the robin and oriole come to see
    The red maple and hawthorn blow.

And the south-wind, far from over the Lake,
    Seems babbling of by-gone years,—
And the purple sky is bending low,
    All smiles and happy tears.

And I stalk a-field, a Scottish Bard,
    To reel the rustic rhyme,—
When in a moment I seem to be
    Where Teviot's waters chime !
And high above the gowany lea,
    The Laverock soars and sings ;—
And Jeanie, I wad that they were here
    To glorify our Springs !

We have meadows where he'd make his nest,
    And skies where he'd like to sing ;—
As sweet and pure as ever felt
    The beating of his wing.
And friendly eyes to follow fond
    His lessening form in air,—
Then, swimming, turn to bless the hand
    That brought the birdie there !

O ye wha leave your native land—
    Howe'er sae little your gear—
To follow the shine o' the setting sun,
    O bring a wheen Laverocks here !
And gie them their liberty fair and free—
    'Tis the land of the free and the true !—
And the Laverock will sing to our bairns' bairns,
    A blessing for me and for you !

We've wandered away to Western skies,
    And planted in precious soil
The love and the lear, the true and the fair,
    That bloomed in our forefathers' Isle!
But the sweet sweet harp of the groves and fields
    Has ever some silent strings,—
For we miss the blythe spirit that early soars,
    With the dew on his flittering wings!

SONG: THE BUSH ABOON TRAQUAIR.

The bonnie bush aboon Traquair,
    Though twined of all its glory,
Yet lives in many an ancient air,
    And many a touching story.
I laid me down to dream my dream
    Of memories sweet and olden;—
And Quair was still a sacred stream,
    And all its air was golden!

A shadow fell upon the bent;
    And ere I could recall me,
Two lovely eyes their witchery lent
    To dazzle and enthral me.
"Kind Sir, your pardon pray command;
    For, my weak fears prevailing,
So long you leaned upon your hand,
    I feared that you were ailing."

The bonnie bush aboon Traquair
    Regained its pristine glory ;
As in that soft and sunset air
    Love lisped his oft-told story !
The blossoms breathed a fa'rer May—
    The hillsides caught the splendor—
As there, in guise of ancient lay,
    I urged the tale so tender.

And now when Spring is on the hills,
    And Hope her tale is telling,
We wander forth to mark the rills
    That gentle Quair are swelling :—
And say no scene is half so fair
    As where we met together ;—
The bonnie bush aboon Traquair,
    And that sweet summer weather !

THE GHOST THAT DANCED AT JETHART.

When guid King Aylsander was marriet—
    'Twas langsyne, kimmer, i' the town o' Jethart ;
Stane-biggit, Abbey-crowned, auld Border clachan,
Whiles I hae thought o' greetin', and whiles lauchin',
    Just as fond memory wi' the past forgather't,
And down Time's stream was carriet.

The King strode through the Abbey Hall,
   Wi' the stride o' a battle-field ;
He was neither a callant to mind your call,
   Nor yet was a man o' eild !
But a man—we never saw but ane,
   Nor ever saw him more !—
The king we wis't for aye could reign—
And the gentle queen on his arm remain,
A treasured jewel in joy and pain—
And gladness come to ilk hame again—
   The braid land o'er !

And at his knee the courtiers bowed,
   And gentle ladies fair ;—
Nor kent that monk and Abbot grumbled loud,
That a' the town had come, a loyal crowd,
   To bend the knee, and then a measure take—
A generous dance, wi' lord and lady in't—
And landward lassie fresh frae pu'in' lint ;
   A' merry for his sake !

But the king said, " Every ane enjoy his sel' !
   For a king's no marriet every day !
And the only thing a man can tell,
   Is, *Tak the sunshine while ye may*.'"

When guid King Aylsander was marriet,
   The provost, and the baillies o' the town,
The waukers, wabsters, and the smiths and souters,
The merchants, millers, and the caudron-clouters,
   And every cadger frae the kintra roun',
Wad celebrate The Weddin' !

And a' the town was ta'en wi' dancin'—
   Frae the Town-fit to the Abbey !
A' dancin' to the weel-being o' the king !—
   And Ringan Hastie cam,
The first town-piper o' the ancient borough—
   And a lang lad wi' a bassoon yet langer,
   And whillie-wha's, and instruments o' clangor,
And kettle-drums, and fifes to pierce lugs thorough,
And harps, and men to sing!

And the King sate at his marriage-feast,
   Wi' the queen at his left han',
And lords and ladies gather't there,
Round the table heaped wi' dainty fare,
And that stretched awa' to the outer air !
(And wha couldna fin' a seat to spare,
   Gat ilk ane's leave to stan' !)

Then flowed the yill, as large as Jed in simmer !
   And whangs o' cheese and bannocks,
High towered in air alang the groanin' board,
Wi' pears and epples frae the carefu' hoard
   O' burgess loyal ;
And haggis, tripe, and every dainty stored
   For feast sae royal !

Then, like a hailstorm through the forest grand,
   A rushing dinnle,
Began the dance, sworn to keep on till morn ;—
E'en crazy eild until the swirl was borne,—
   And, " JETHART'S HERE!" roared out bow-legged
     Tam Tinnle—
When sudden cam a stand !

But still the patter o' a pair o' feet
    Was heard fu' right !
The lad had fainted wi' the lang bassoon,
And kettle-drums and fifes were in a swoon—
    And harpers glowered atween their silent thairms
      On sic a sight !

It jousl't wi' its elbucks e'en the king—
    And maskers fled,—
For ne'er in masquerade had sic a thing
    Been seen or read !
It wasna' leevin', yet 'twas dancin', loupin',
And over the provost it was nearly coupin',
    Sic whirls it led !

It had a plume as it had been a baron,
    Wi' feathers hie, —
A kilt wi' gold brocade and siller lacing',—
And dainty doublet wi' a braw, braw facin',
    But *hon-och-rie !*
It was an *atomy*, a thing o' banes,
    That wadna' dee.

It lightly trod the airy min-e-wae,
    And crackt its fleshless thoombs ;
And linked wi' unseen partners down the floor,
As country-dance was never danced before !
    And girned and boo'd to ladies on the dais,
      Then flittit frae the place !

"Ho! Tam the Tip!" cried out the provost bald,
  "Bring back yon loon!
We'll pit him whaur he winna be sae yauld,
And gie him time to blaw his parritch cauld;
  He might hae hid his banes wi' decent garb—
  Affronting the town!"

But ne'er was seen yon merrie Ghost again
  In Jethart dear!
Her battle-axes fell on Southron shields,
Her sturdy spearmen won victorious fields,—
  And "JETHART'S HERE!"
Rang down the ages, as the battle-plain
  Its heroes gather't;—
But one, and only one, shall that remain,
  The GHOST o' JETHART!

NOTE.—I have not invented this ghost. I find it narrated, as something that would be the better of explanation—but has never been explained—that at a masquerade ball given in Jedburgh, 1285, at the marriage there of King Alexander III, a ghost danced! Sir Michael Scott (the "Wizard,") who was then living, was the best man to have explained it; but though he wrote about everything—rams' flesh, and bishops—pot-herbs and wicked women—kings and emperors, and roasting of eggs—the dignity of friendship, and whether fishes chew their food—he has not told us a word in explanation of "The Ghost that danced at Jethart!" It was perhaps a pious fraud of the Abbot and the monks, not well-pleased at so much hilarity in the Abbey. Hector Boece distinctly says, "A Skeleton danced."—W. W. S.

SONG: "GIN YE CANNA GIE THE PUND."

Gin ye canna gie the pund,
    Still the penny gie him;
Gin ye canna save a freend,
    Ye may suffer wi' him.
Gin ye canna as ye wad,
    Still do as ye may;
Sit na doun to wyte nor wuss,
    Tak the thing ye hae!

Ance langsyne cam English loons
    Ower the Border reavin',
Louped the Laird o' Langton there,
    Intill his saddle screavin';
"I hae nae mail," quo' he, "the day,
    I'll turn my coat instead o't;
They'll think I hae my jack-proof on,
    An' rin for vera dread o't!"

Wait nae mair on Fortune's smile—
    She's a heartless limmer!
Sit na doun wi' broken branks—
    Whyte the nearest timmer!
Bide nae holes in a' your pouch,
    Though toom till heart be sair;
Hae a guid word for yoursel',—
    Ithers learn the lear!

Mony a time King Robert rued
    Hauberk, helm and whinger;
Sad and sair that Freedom's fecht
    Should dool and sorrow bring her.
But aye he fought, and aye he sought,
    Till Bannockburn rewardit;
The King as crouse to win his crown
    As Minstrel to record it!

SONG: THE BIRDIE THAT'S WANTIN' A WING.

They say there's a birdie that's wantin' a wing,
    Ower the sea; ower the sea;—
He neither can flie, nor yet can he sing,
    Ower the sea; ower the sea.
But he finds him a mate—sae he's no sae bereft—
He has a right wing, and she has a left—
And they link on thegither, and aff they gae daft
    Ower the sea; ower the sea!

They say there's a birdie that's wantin' a note,
    Ower the sea; ower the sea;—
And a' the high sounds seem to stick in his throat—
    Ower the sea; ower the sea.
But he finds him a mate wi' the high notes sae clear—
He has the *bass*, and she has the *air*—
And, "Turn about, Tibbie!" the sang's rich and rare!
    Ower the sea; ower the sea.

I tell't it to Kate ; and I thought I was slee,
    By the dyke-stane ; by the dyke-stane ;—
And in the bit birdie I hoped she'd see me,
    Dowie and fain ; dowie and fain.
" It was a daft ditty," she said, " she must say ;
And when a chield tauld his love-tale in that way,
She thought it was time that he let his tongue play,
    And spak his mind plain ; and spak his mind plain !"

O, the Sun it cam out, and the birds they sang clear !
    Ower the lea ; ower the lea !
And the lass that I lo'ed seemed never sae dear
    Ever to me ; ever to me !
The wing that was wantin', I faund it complete—
The sang that was mantin' was perfect and sweet !
And twa Scottish lovers, twa hearts wi' ae beat,
    Sat there by the sea ; sat there by the sea !

Religious.

": I will sing you a song of that beautiful land,
　　The far-away home of the soul,—
　Where no storms ever beat on the glittering strand
　　While the years of eternity roll!"

　　　　　　　　　　—ELLEN H. GATES.

Religious.

I CAME, BUT I CAME WITH MYSELF.

I CAME, but I came with myself,—
   With my deeds that were doing or done ;
With the half-finished strife of a purified life,
   But never God's crucified Son !

I came, but I came with my tears,—
   Lamenting the sins I abhorred ;—
With penitent sighs, and with sorrowful eyes,
   But never the Cross of my Lord !

I came, but I came with my vows,—
   I never would wander again !
And the hope that I had was the promise I made,
   But never the Lamb that was slain !

I came with my Saviour and Lord ;—
   Not a claim, nor a hope, nor a plea
But Jesus hath died, and the Law satisfied !
   And the dying and debt were for me !

I cling to my crucified Lord,—
   And the path of the pilgrim is blest ;
And his name is the plea that will open to me
   The way to the Kingdom of Rest !

THE MERITS OF CHRIST FOR NOTHING.

"The merits of Christ for nothing ; large, and white, and fair."
                              Samuel Rutherford.

   The merits of Christ for nothing,
      Large, and white, and fair !
   I am bidden to come to the Supper,
      And that is the robe I'll wear !
   Woven in light—pure and white—
      A princely robe to bear ;—
   The merits of Christ for nothing,—
      Large, and white, and fair !

   He'll honor the robe he gave me
      With his own royal hand ;
   And smile when he sees me enter
      As one of his ransomed band.
   Children of light ! clothed in white !
      As in your ranks I stand—
   He'll honor the robe he gave me
      With his own royal hand.

The sweetest hope I have cherished
  Is now to be saved by grace ;—
That vainest of hopes has perished—
  Through works to see God's face !
The robe of Christ—his worth unpriced—
  Here all my trust I place :—
The sweetest hope I have cherished
  Is now to be saved by grace !

THE CROSS-BEARER.

His Lord gave Caer a cross to carry ;
  And, pointing to the distant blue,
He bade him neither turn nor tarry,
  But haste the Stranger-Country through !
" And I will meet thee at the portal
  Where grief goes out, and bliss begins ;
And thou with me shalt dwell, immortal,
  A sinner saved from all his sins ! "

And Caer marched on with warbling snatches
  Of Salem's songs, clear-sounding high ;
And oft his airy fancy catches
  A glimpse of glory from the sky.
Till in the vale, a band pursuing,
  Fierce and far, surround him there ;
And loud demanded his undoing,
  And what and whence the load he bare ?

And Caer laid down, with bosom swelling,
  The cross, so heavy now for him ;—
"A beam," he said, "to make a dwelling,
  He hewed beside the river's brim !"
Then rose the shout of sinners scorning ;
  They took his cross, they beat him there—
And left him lying, lowly mourning.
  A *crossless sinner* in despair !

Then came his Lord, at midnight starry,—
  Forgave him, kissed him, calmed his strife :
And gave him back his cross to carry—
  "O leave it only with thy life !"
Once more the Stranger-Country threading,
  He watches more, if less he sings,—
Himself as well as aliens dreading
  He to his burden closer clings !

Last eve he passed, with cross uplifted,—
  His eyes were sunk, his lips were firm ;
And I need scarce be Prophet-gifted
  To see him safe from snare and storm !
O Saint within the Eternal morrow !
  I too would go where glory waits ;—
And learn, as thou, without thy sorrow,
  The cross to carry to the gates !

COME, O COME, THOU KING ETERNAL!

Come, O come, thou King Eternal,
    Over us and all to reign!
Let the Spring, with blossoms vernal,
    Visit our poor hearts again!
O for love so pure and fervent—
    Love reflected from thy throne—
As to find each happy servant
    Living for his Lord alone!

'Tis afar, and yet 'tis present,
    'Tis on high, and yet 'tis mine—
Every comfort, sweet and pleasant,
    Jesus gives of joy divine.
Oh, I would these hands could crown him!
    Oh, I would these eyes could see,
And this voice with raptures own him
    Source of every bliss to me."

Yet my Lord comes whispering to me,
    "This, and more, shall all be thine!"
Sin, though strong, shall not undo me,
    Resting on his arm divine.
So I wait a little longer
    For his fellowship above;
Yearning with a holy hunger
    For the perfectness of love!

BETTER THAN ALL.

I would love Christ the best of all ;
  His presence my poor soul uplifts :—
His smile is sweeter than my joy—
  The Bridegroom better than his gifts !

I make no more my joy or boast
  In fervid frames, or aught my own :
They are but golden gifts at most,
  The King's more kingly than his crown !

Himself most glorious of his gifts—
  Abiding bliss, without alloy :
One smile of his my soul uplifts,
  For Christ is better than my joy !

Better than love ; better than joy ;
  Better than earth and Heaven the whole,—
For Christ to come and make his home
  In the poor dwelling of my soul.

I HAD ONE FOR AN ENEMY.

I had one for an enemy ;
Yet I loved him, for God loved me ;—
He came within my way, and I
Did good for evil still supply.
And so I gained him for a friend,
And so his hatred found an end ;
And soft the Spirit said to me,
" Thus did thy Saviour conquer thee ! "

Thus David spared the life of Saul,
When in his hands the King did fall ;
And made him in confession cry,
" Thou art more righteous far, than I ! "
Thus Christ with love and pity smiled
On him who from his cross reviled ;
And won the thief, all tears and cries,
To go with him to Paradise.

O gentle love, that conquers hate !
O sweetest word at Heaven's gate !
O let my soul be filled with thee,
That I may soon my Saviour see !
My foes alone, the foes of God—
Friends, all who yearn for thine abode—
My hope, the promise from above—
My home, the bosom of thy love !

WHEN YOU GET HOME.

When you get home to the fields of glory,
   What will you wear? What will you wear?
I'll wear the white robe that my Saviour prepares —
As white as the truth, and as bright as the stars;
And rent with no sorrows, and stained with no tears—
   That will I wear; that will I wear!

When you get home to your Father's mansion,
   What will you see? What will you see?
I'll see the great light of His glorious throne,—
The face of The Blessed who sits thereupon—
The Angels of Light, and the Saints gathered home—
   That will I see; that will I see!

When you get home to the Land of Angels,
   What will you hear? What will you hear?
The harps and the anthems of heavenly joy—
The blessings that ever our tongues shall employ—
And voices of Angels ascending on high—
   That will I hear; that will I hear!

When you get home to the Rest of Jesus,
   What will you say? What will you say?
I'll tell him I've come, for I've heard his blest word:
I'll tell him I'm here, for to follow my Lord;
That hope now is vision, and promise reward—
   That will I say; that will I say!

When you get home to that blessed harbor,
  Who will be there ? Who will be there ?
All, all who have loved with the Saviour to be—
All, all whom my spirit is yearning to see—
And all I have loved, and who learned to love me—
  They will be there ; they will be there !

When you get home, and your journey ended,
  What will you do ? What will you do ?
I'll fall at his feet who has bled and has died,
I'll put on the badge of the Once-Crucified—
I'll tarry forever at his blessed side—
That will I do ; that will I do !

MY HEAVENLY FRIEND.

My Lord comes down, so friendly, free,
  And all my pain beguileth ;
And when I weep, he weeps with me—
  And when I'm glad, he smileth.

Before I felt his love at first,
  I grieved him oft in blindness ;
But now of all my wounds 'tis worst
  To sin against his kindness.

And blessing thus my life's estate,
  Dark days, or sunshine vernal—
He'll not desert me at the gate
  That leads to life Eternal !

BETHEL.

Where'er Jehovah meets my soul
    A Bethel is to me !
The parted clouds asunder roll
    And Paradise I see.

The feeble prayer I faintly breathed
    I see ascend on high ;
And heavenly blessings round it wreathed
    Descend the glowing sky.

Like Jacob 'neath the lonely stars,
    My pillow but a stone—
If God the gate of heaven unbars,
    My sorrows all are gone !

Faith's ladder reaches to the sky ;
    And blessings there descend ;—
All praise to Him who brings us nigh,—
    My ever-blessed Friend !

                          Gen. 28 : 10-17.

THE SONG OF MOSES.

O sing to the Lord, He hath triumphed in glory !
   The rider and steed hath he cast in the sea !
The Lord is my strength, and the song of my story;
   My help and my Saviour forever is he.

The Lord is my God ; in a high habitation
   The God of my fathers exalted shall be !
The Lord maketh war ! in his name is salvation !
   The chariot and host he hath cast in the sea !

The Captains, outbreathing oppression and slaughters,
   Are drowned in the depths of the ocean below;—
As a stone, so they sank in the midst of the waters!
   God's hand hath all shattered the might of the foe !

The foes that withstood thee but flourished to wither—
   Consumed as the stubble that burns in thy path;—
At thy breath were the waters all gathered together,
   And the pulse of the deep became silent as death !

Then madly the enemy rushed to the slaughter—
   To the spoil and revenge, and to glory untold;—
Thou didst blow with thy wind, and beneath that wild
      water
   Like lead they lay sunken, as lifeless and cold !

Who is like unto thee, O thou mighty in glory?
  Or who 'mong the gods is compared unto thee?—
All holy and glorious, wondrous in story;—
  Thou only our praise and redemption shall be!

Ex. xv.

GOD OF GLORY.

God of Glory! let me be
Still a worshipper of thee!
Let thy glory and thy love,
Beaming from the heaven above,
Lead the soul thou dost make free,
Still to worship only thee!

God of Grace! thy name shall be
Honored to Eternity!—
For the gift of Jesus' love—
For the hopes of heaven above!—
Ever blest thy name shall be,—
Honored to Eternity!

God of Love! thy holy day
Teaches us to praise and pray;—
Like a foretaste from the sky,
Of an endless day on high;—
So let every Sabbath day
Teach us how to praise and pray!

Ex. xx. 3-11

CHRIST, THE ONLY PRIEST.

Altar and sacrifice,
   Vanished away;
Nothing before my eyes
   Now when I pray :—
Only I know that he,
Dying, who died for me
   Takes sin away!

Temple, and waiting priest,
   Now find I none;
Offering, and holy feast,
   All, all are gone!
Christ in my room and stead,
Christ for my Heavenly Bread,
   Christ mine alone!

I have no offering,
   Pardon to win;
Only a soul I bring,
   Weary of sin!
High Priest before the Throne,
Thou art my trust alone ;—
   Lord, take me in!

                Lev. i.

MOSES.

Up from the Plains of Moab he went,
  To Nebo's mountain bare:
And on the top of Pisgah bent
  Before Jehovah there!
While o'er the Plains of Jericho,
  And o'er the Jordan deep,
The long-sought Land of Promise lay
  Like rapture in a sleep!

He looked on Gilead's hills of blue,
  To farthest bounds of Dan;—
From Naphtali his raptured view
  To Ephraim's mountains ran:—
Manasseh's portion, yet to be,
  And Judah's regal land;
From the far gleam of utmost sea,
  To Zoar at his left hand.

"This is the land," Jehovah said,
  "That I to Abraham sware
Should, by his seed inherited,
  Above all lands be fair.
And thou hast seen it with thine eyes,
  My faithful word to know,—
But o'er that stream that hidden lies
  Thou shalt not thither go."

Then fades the wondrous vision bright
   Before his weary eyes;
And dead upon Mount Nebo's height
   Within God's hand he lies.
And had for pageant burial,
   And a tomb with garlands drest,—
A rest unseen in a vale of green,
   And a home among the blest!

Deut. xxxiv.

THE MOUNT OF VISION.

As Moses sang his Song of Songs,
To Him to whom the praise belongs,
And charged the host that round him stood,
To shun the ill, and choose the good;—
So our Great Leader breathed a prayer
For us, for mankind everywhere;—
Then heard, like him, the voice on high—
Like him went up the Mount to die!

And from that mountain saw he there
The land that God to Abraham sware,
From Gilead's mountains far and free,
O'er Judah to the utmost sea.
And from his Cross shall Jesus view
The World his grace creates anew;
And die, with glory in his soul
That man may rise from sin's control!

And oh, when we our portion see,
From Nebo's top, or Calvary,
Then what is death, that comes between!
A margin-line across the scene!
And there beyond, our treasure lies,
With balmy air and sunny skies—
And we, where Sin hath never trod,
Shall be at home, and walk with God.
—Deut. 34.

ISRAEL CROSSING JORDAN.

The desert was all behind them,
    The weariness and the pain ;—
The Land lay all before them,
    Across the river-plain.
The yellow corn-fields waving,
    The vineyards clad in green ;
Seemed beckoning onward to that host,
    Where Jordan lay between.

They thought not of the harvest
    That swelled the floods between—
They thought but of the harvest
    All bright in golden sheen.
'Tis thus when Heaven comes o'er us,
    Its glory and its power,
Death has no terrors, Earth no claims—
    Our Home lies just before!

They harnessed for the battle,
   To fight the foes of God;
Wherever he led onward,
   With willing feet they trod.
Oh, when the Lord doth promise
   A land of blissful rest,
Our waiting souls already share
   The rapture of the Blest!

Lead on, thou glorious Chieftain!
   To conquest over sin;—
And follow, ye his people,
   Your heritage to win!
A greater far than Joshua
   Has passed, our tents among,—
Saying, "Be thou strong and full of faith:
   Thy toil shall end in song!"

The Ark went down before them—
   The sweeping billows stood;—
No man had ever dared to stem
   That raging harvest-flood.
Yet white-robed priests went meekly
   Adown the slippery steep,
And gathered round the Ark of God—
   That wondrous path to keep.

So when Death's swelling billow
   My feet essay at last,
The Ark goes down before me,
   And stays till I have passed.

The waters "heap" above me,
　　The waters "fail" below—
And to the Land my God bestows,
　　My happy footsteps go.

Ah, firm my High-Priest resteth
　　Beside the Ark of God;
Till e'en the weakest pilgrim
　　On Canaan's shore hath trod.
He leads us as we enter,
　　He cheers us as we go:
He leads us—comes behind us—
　　And guards from every foe!

There were some who well remembered
　　How they passed the Red Sea through:
And how sank the hosts of Pharaoh,
　　Before their childish view.
And the same Lord would lead them
　　Through Jordan's lesser flood;—
And strong in faith they passed where firm
　　The Testimony stood!

And they who went in trembling,
　　Starting at every breeze,
Came none the less in safety through
　　By the same power as these.
O Faith that never falters!
　　O Hope that never dies!
Death, that robs us of our courage,
　　Cannot rob us of our prize!

　　　　　　　　　—Josh. 3: and 4.

GO SEEK A MAN IN BETHLEHEM.

"Go seek a man in Bethlehem ;
  A king I name to thee,
And him anoint in midst of them,
  Whose heart is right with me!"
'Twas thus of David God did speak,—
  And him the Prophet found ;
Ruddy, and fair, and young and meek,—
  Whom God with blessings crowned.

"From Bethlehem shall he arise—
  A Prince to rule for God ;—
O look to Him, your Sacrifice,
  All ends of earth abroad !"
'Twas thus of Jesus God did speak,—
  Forever faithful found ;—
Obedient, holy, pure and meek,
  With Heavenly blessings crowned.

He left the flocks of Bethlehem—
  The path of duty trod ;
And gained of praise the diadem—
  "His heart was right with God !"
'Twas thus of David God did speak—
  And him the Prophet found :
Ruddy, and fair, and young and meek,—
  Whom God with blessings crowned.

He left the glorious land above,
    To do thy will, O God !
" And he shall reign in peace and love,
    O'er every land abroad !"
'Twas thus of Jesus God did speak,—
    Forever faithful found ;—
Obedient, holy, pure and meek,—
    With Heavenly blessings crowned.

I. SAM. 16 : 1.

KEEP ME FREE AND PURE!

Thou hast given this life to me---
Life to honor only thee !
But to sit in drunkards' seat,
Makes life ever but defeat !

> *Keep me free ; keep me pure !*
> *Let me to the end endure ;*
> *Every power thou giv'st to me,*
> *Let me render, Lord, to thee !*

Thou hast given a soul to me—
Soul to follow only thee !
But beneath the wine-cup's sway,
Fades its noblest powers away !

    CHO:

Thou hast won a Heaven for me—
Offered freely, oh how free !
But Intemperance' fatal power
Bars the portal evermore !

Cho :

I Kings 20 : 12-16.

ELIJAH.

Worn and weary with Earth's fighting,
　Sighed Elijah for his home,
As he crossed the Jordan's waters,
　Where he knew relief would come !
And the angels bright descended
　To that lonely river shore—
Where the prophet found his glory,
　And the mourner sighed no more.

So Elijah rose to heaven,
　So remained his humble friend ;
One to see his Master's glory,
　One to work till life should end.
Both shall stand at Christ's appearing,
　Both have welcome of their Lord ;
And the soul that follows Jesus
　Has fulfilment of his word.

Not on Carmel was his triumph,
   Though the power of God was there—
When the priests of Baal were smitten
   With destruction and despair :
But 'twas in that lonely valley,
   Just beyond the Jordan's stream,
Where the Prophet had his glory,
   And the dreamer had his dream !

Thus, 'tis not when we're exalted
   On some mountain of renown,
But when humble in the valley
   Comes the chariot rushing down.
Oh, to share that day of triumph,
   When with Christ we rise on high,
With ten thousand times ten thousand,
   To the glories of the sky !

II Kings, 2.

THE LEPER.

Let praise arise to God above,
    The Saviour of my soul;
I came to Him with trembling love,
    And he has made me whole!

My sin was found in every part—
    A leprosy within;
I came with a polluted heart,
    And he forgave my sin!

No Syrian gold, nor raiment white
    Can I on him bestow;
A humble soul, a heart contrite,
    Is all the gift I know.

'Twas God who did the gift bestow,
    'Twas I the gift received;
I dipped into the Jordan's flow,
    And as I laved I lived!

And ever, on my pilgrim path,
    His grace will I extol;
The Father turns away his wrath,
    And Jesus make me whole!

                    II KINGS 5.

BUILDING FOR GOD.

They came to lay the Temple walls,
    And build a house for God :
And raise the sacred ruins up,
    The spoiler long had trod.
Their song the listening stranger heard,
    Upon the hills afar—
" How good and kind art thou, O Lord !
    How great thy mercies are !"

And shouts and sobs alternate broke
    Upon the morning air ;—
They wept to see the ruins lie,
    Yet joyed to labour there.
And joy and sorrow mingled rose,
    And reached the hills afar,—
" How good and kind art thou, O Lord !
    How great thy mercies are ! "

So let us raise the ruined walls
    Our fainting faith deplored ;
And set our broken altars up,
    And vow to serve the Lord !
And, O thou King of Glory, hear,
    Even on thy throne afar,
As here we sing, " How good thou art !
    How great thy mercies are ! "

                  Ezra 3.

THE CURSE OF WINE.

Crown of praise, and glorious beauty,
    Passed away like fading flower !
In the wine-cup, God and duty
    All forgotten in an hour !
        Let Jehovah,
        Let Jehovah,
    Be his people's crown and power !

Prophet, priest, through wine are erring—
    Prayer and faith are faint and low ;
And the church of God is bearing
    Pain upon her saintly brow !
        Lord, deliver !
        Lord, deliver !
    Save from sin, and save us now !

Brighter days, and days of glory
    Rise, when God shall Zion crown ;—
When the wine-cup's dismal story
    Dims no more her fair renown !
        Lord of glory,
        Lord of glory,
    Reign thou o'er the world alone !

                Is. 28 : 1-17.

AWAKE, AWAKE, O ZION!

Awake, awake, O Zion!
   In strength and glory sing!
Put on thy robe of beauty,
With holy joy and duty,—
   Thou city of the King!
   Thou city of the King!

Thy bondage and thy mourning
   Shall pass like night away
No more, the foe oppressing ;—
But God thy wrongs redressing ;—
   Thy darkness turns to day!
   Thy darkness turns to day!

The heralds of salvation,
   How beautiful their feet!
Upon the mountains flying,—
With news to sinners dying,
   Their ransom is complete!
   Their ransom is complete!

The voice of watchmen singing,
   On every breeze is blown ;—
With eye to eye beholding,
The glorious day unfolding,
   When Christ shall reign alone!
   When Christ shall reign alone!

Our God in might arising,
   Hath bared his arm and cried,
"Ho, ye of every nation!
   Return, and taste salvation ;
     For Christ, your Lord, **hath died!**"
     *For Christ, your Lord, **hath died!***

Is. 52 : 1-10.

GOD RESTORING.

God's great voice afar is sounding,
   I, the Lord, will be thy God!
They who fled from sword and slaughter,
Shall to me be son and daughter,
    Ev'n in silent wilderness—
    Where my peace doth Israel bless!

Lo, of old the Lord appearing ;—
   Mine is everlasting love!
All my loving kindness thrilled thee—
Once again, O Land, I build thee !—
    Decked with jewels—crowned with song,
    Thou shalt join the joyful throng.

On Samaria's silent mountains
   Shall the vine her clusters fill ;—
Thou shalt plant and thou shalt eat them ;

And her watchmen, thou shall greet them,
   On Mount Ephraim, crying loud,
   Come to Zion ! come to God !

Saith the Lord, O sing for Israel !
   Shout, among the nations shout !
Praise thy glorious God and Father,
Say, O Lord, thy people gather !
   Save, O save the remnant small !
   Helpless at thy feet we fall.

From the North afar I bring them,
   Shining gems from every shore ;—
Poor, and weak, and blind and weeping,
Come they home in God's own keeping !
   Glad, as never glad before—
   God their Father, evermore !

Jer. 31 : 1-9.

EARTH'S JUBILEE.

O Mountain of the Mercy Seat !
   How great thy glories are !
In latter days, when thou shalt rise,
   Exalted from afar !
O dawning day, we wait for thee !
Thou day of peace, Earth's Jubilee !

The tribes of Earth, from every land,
  Like gathering seas shall flow,
To seek the Lord, and learn his ways,
  And of his glory know.
    Cho :

And from her tears shall Zion rise ;
  And all her sorrows cease ;
And glorious in the nations' eyes
  Exalt the Prince of Peace !
    Cho :

They'll beat their swords to plowshares then ;
  To pruning-hooks their spears ;—
And Peace come down to dwell with men
  Through the long tranquil years.
    Cho :

And meekly, 'neath his sheltering vine,
  The pious poor shall rest ;
For God hath sworn no foe shall rise,
  Nor sound of war molest.
    Cho :

O Salem's King ! thy reign begin !
  Bring all thy banished home ;—
And Earth shall bloom beneath thy smile ;—
  O come, thou Saviour, come !
    Cho :

Micah 4 : 1-7.

TEMPTATIONS.

Defend me from my foes, O God !
    Defend me from my foes !
He who unharmed the desert trod,
    The desert-trial knows.
When Satan takes my lack of wealth
    To make me doubt thy power,—
My lack of bread, or lack of health—
    Defend me in that hour !

Keep me from earthly pride, O God !
    Keep me from earthly pride !
For oft the Tempter shows abroad
    False glories far and wide.
O be the kingdom that I seek,
    My glory and my grace,
The kingdom of the poor and meek,
    The smiling of thy face !

I would not doubt thy power, O God !
    I would not doubt thy power !
Nor tempt the terrors of thy rod
    With rashness of an hour !
Enough to know thou wilt surround
    With strength thy weakest child,—
And lead him safe to Salem's ground,
    Through dangers dark and wild.

                      Matt. 4: 1-11.

BLESSED!

Blessed, blessed! Poor in spirit,
   Mourning, weeping all the day;—
Yours a kingdom to inherit—
   God shall wipe your tears away!
Blessed, blessed! Meek and lowly,
   You from rage and strife afar,—
Earth is yours, and Heaven so holy;
   You shall shine where angels are!

Blessed, blessed! Hungering, thirsting
   For the righteousness you love;
Lo, for you the fount is bursting,
   And the feast awaits Above.
Blessed, blessed! kind, forgiving,—
   In the smile of God you rest;
Mercy from on High receiving—
   Blessed now, and ever blest!

Blessed, blessed! O pure-hearted,
   Ye who make, and live for peace!
You from God shall ne'er be parted,
   Nor from you his favor cease.
Blessed thou for Truth who diest—
   Persecuted, trembling, tried—
Thine the kingdom of the Highest,
   Thine the smile of him who died!

                      Matt. 5: 3-12.

THE LORD'S PRAYER.

Father, O Father! whose home is in Heaven,
Hallowed and blest be the name thou hast given!
Here may thy kingdom, we pray, have its birth;
And as in Heaven, thy will be on Earth.

Give us the bread by which daily we live;
Grant us forgiveness, for we too forgive;—
Lead not to trials, but save us from sin :—
Thine is the kingdom, forever, Amen!

THE TWO WAYS.

O broad and fair the garnished gate
    The many enter in;—
But lurid is their lost estate
    Who walk the ways of sin!
The heartless jest, the ribald song,
    The light and wanton eye
Are ever there, but in the throng
    Despair is lurking nigh.

O who would win the wealth of sin,
    To sink in sin's despair?
Or who would seek to enter in,
    When Jesus says, " Beware!"
Away, away from downward road,
    That leads from peace afar!
And upward seek the Saints' abode,
    Where Christ and glory are!

For narrow is the gate that keeps
    Eternal life within ;
And rugged are the sacred steeps
    That lead afar from sin !
There lead us, O thou loving Guide,
    Through holiness to thee !
That at the blessed Saviour's side
    Our rest may ever be !
Matt. 7 : 13, 14.

HOUSE ON THE ROCK.

O House on the rock, be my dwelling in thee !
Deep founded in faith on his promise to me ;—
Each stone be some act or some thought purified,—
Each beam like the cross of my Saviour who died !

They mocked me, and said it was toilsome and vain,
And bade me go build on the sand of the plain ;—
But surely if safety myself could provide,
That Rock had not risen, and Christ had not died !

When floods in their fury came down to devour,
My Rock is my refuge, for Jesus has power ;—
While wrecks I behold on the billows abroad,
All safe on the Rock I am dwelling with God !
Matt. 7 : 24-27.

THERE'S A BOAT HAS LAUNCHED AWAY.

There's a boat has launched away,
   But the blessed Master's in it;—
There's a soul set out to-day,
   Seeking Heaven, and fain would win it.
But the boat shall not be lost,
Nor the soul's endeavour crossed,—
   For Jesus came to save poor sinners!

There's a storm upon the sea,
   And the boat is wildly tossing;—
There's a soul that would be free,
   Through some dark temptation crossing:—
But the boat is shattered not,
Nor the tempted soul forgot—
   For Jesus came to save poor sinners!

There's a voice that calms the sea,
   And the waves have ceased their raging;
There's a voice that speaks to me,
   All my pain of soul assuaging:—
"HAVE THOU FAITH!" the Saviour cries,
"I BELIEVE!" my soul replies,
   For Jesus came to save poor sinners!

                        Matt. 8: 23-27.

COME TO THE SAVIOUR, COME!

Come to the Cross, ye sad and forsaken;
    Weary and wandering, come!
Out of your lethargy leap and awaken,—
    Sunken and silent and dumb.
Come with your follies, and come with your fears,
Come with your turnings, your terrors and tears,
Come with the sorrows and strivings of years,—
    Come to the Saviour, come!

Take up the yoke, and wear it with pleasure;
    Learn of the Saviour well
How tribulation he turns into treasure,
    Greater than tongue can tell!
Learn of the Lowly, the Pure and the Meek,—
Learn how he keepeth the rest that you seek—
Burdens he bears for the worn and the weak;
    Come to the Saviour, come!

Light is the load when his grace goes with it,—
    Leader, and Lover and Friend!
Sweet is the rest with his love beneath it,
    Solace that never shall end!
Come to the Refuge, and you shall have rest,
Come to the Blessed, and you shall be blest!
Now and forever a friend and a guest;—
    Come to the Saviour, come!

                —Matt. xi. 28-30.

TRANSFIGURED.

O mountain of mercy, where Jesus shone forth
As the Son of the Highest, the Lord of the Earth !
How oft on thy summit my spirit would be,
Apart from the World, blessed Saviour, with thee !

Thy face was transfigured from sorrow and pain,
And shone as when high over all thou didst reign ;
Thy raiment was whiter than Seraphim wear,
And the Saints of the sky were thy visitants there !

And Prophet and Leader with wonder begin
To speak of the death that redeems us from sin ;
And a voice from the brightness sounds solemn and clear,
" My Son ! My Beloved one ! Him shall ye hear !"

And like the disciples, all prone to the earth,
We fall on our face as thy glory shines forth ;—
O say to our souls, that our sorrows shall cease,
" Arise ye, and fear not ; in me ye have peace !"

—Matt. xvii. 1-7.

AT THE TREASURY.

Jesus beside the Treasury sat,
   And marked the givers as they passed;
How great was this, and greater that,
   The rich into the Treasury cast.

And many whom the Lord had given
   The wealth of Earth, and golden store,
Thought they discharged their debt to Heaven
   When their large gifts they proudly pour.

But, unobservant of the proud,
   And seen by him she loved, alone,
Lo, a poor widow in the crowd
   Hath her two mites in meekness thrown.

"And this," said he, whose balance weighs
   The gold against the giver's thought,
"With me hath honor more, and praise,
   Than all the gifts that these hath brought!"

O Lord, and dost thou still observe
   The gifts thy people bring to thee?
Then let me still my Saviour serve,
   And every thought an offering be!

—Mark xii. 41-44.

TRUE REPENTANCE.

All men coming, heard at Jordan,
   John the great Forerunner say,
" Bear the fruits of true Repentance,
   And your life its deeds display !
Let whate'er your hands are doing
   Show the heart renewed within ;—
Love, and life, and peace pursuing,—
   Fruits of faith, afar from sin !

" Let the needy, lacking raiment,
   From thine open hand receive ;
Thou shalt have in over-payment
   Peace that God alone can give.
Break thy bread to feed the hungry,—
   Ask, thyself, for living bread !
He, of every gift the Giver,
   Shall send blessings on thy head !"

Lord, baptize us with thy Spirit !
   Let us feel the holy fire !
Life Eternal all inherit,—
   Pure reward of pure desire !
And when thou, in Judgment coming,
   Shalt the chaff drive from thy floor,
Safe within thy garner gathered,
   May we be for evermore !

                —Luke iii. 8-17.

HOLY SAVIOUR, HEAVENLY BREAD!

Holy Saviour, heavenly bread!
Thou by whom our souls are fed,
In the desert we shall see
How thou didst from hunger free
Those who followed thee below,
Heard thee, would not let thee go;—
And to us, who would be fed,
Give the living, heavenly bread!

Thousands ate the wondrous bread,
Never reaped by harvest blade;
Thousands wished it more and more—
(Better than all bread before!)
Followed thee across the sea,
'Mid thy mighty works to be;—
Lord, to us who would be fed,
Give the living, heavenly bread!

Keep us free from earthly leaven;
Send our souls the bread of heaven;
Far from hatred, far from pride,
We would seek no bread beside!
Daily let us sit with thee,
Joyful with thy company;—
Lord, to us who would be fed,
Give the living, heavenly bread!

—Luke ix. 11-17.

GO FORTH, GO FORTH, YE CHOSEN!

Go forth, go forth, ye chosen;
    Your message bear with might
To men in darkness waiting,—
    And lead them to the light!
Go tell them God remembers
    His covenant of old,
And doth his blessed Kingdom
    From day to day unfold.

Go preach to men Repentance,
    To save them from their sin;
That souls for heaven longing
    May learn to enter in;—
And if, your word receiving,
    They bless you for its sake,
The freely-offered kindness
    All thankfully partake.

But if, the grace refusing,
    They turn away their eyes,—
And, hating first the message,
    The messengers despise,
Shake off at your departing
    The dust upon your feet,
And carry forth your message
    Where others find it sweet.

Thus fared they forth, to conquer
  The world for Christ the Lord;
And *we* have heard the message,
  And *we* have known the word.
Lord, lead us to receive it
  Within our heart of hearts,
And reign thou ever o'er us
  When time itself departs!
                                    —Luke x. 1-20.

THE LEPERS.

Ten had the leprosy; one had love;
  Ten the Lord cured, but one gave praise:
Ten had the blessing, their sorrows redressing—
  One came to worship, the nine went their ways.

Some are the Lord's, a few in the earth—
  Yet for the whole was the Ransom divine;—
Earth has the blessing; but only confessing
  One 'mong the many found—"Where are the nine?"

Jesus, my Saviour! a stranger am I;
  Leprous my soul with incurable woe;—
Oh to my pleading give merciful heeding,—
  Stranger and friendless—a blessing bestow!

Now to my soul comes healing and balm;—
  Spoken the blessing—the blessing is mine!
Let me, returning, with gratitude burning,
  Low in his presence proclaim him divine!
                                    —Luke xvii. 11-19.

JESUS RISEN.

All hasty and hurried came Peter and John,—
"The tomb has been rifled! The Master is gone!"
In their hot indignation and trouble and awe,
'Twas darkness and emptiness only they saw.

O hearts that are hardened, and eyes that are blind!
Why seek ye the Sepulchre, Jesus to find?
The dead-clothes are there, and the light struggling in,
But *there* is no Saviour who suffered for sin!

He is robed! He is risen! The grave cannot hold
The Conqu'ror of sin, the great Guard of the fold!
He has gone up on high, and again has come down
For a few fleeting hours, ere he puts on his crown!

O Saviour! O Blessed! a visit give me,
And raise to a flame my devotion to thee!
One glance at thy hands, at thy side, at thy brow,
Would prostrate my soul, as I prostrate me now!

But oh, to the heart that is humble and true,
Thy tomb's ever empty, thy rising is new!
Any thou to my soul dost as truly come near,
As when the Eleven beheld thee appear!

So, when I seek Christ, 'twill not be at the tomb;
For a Christ that is *dead* in my heart has no room;—
But I look for a Christ that is living for me,
Who dieth no more, and whom soon I shall see!

—John xx. 1-9.

NOW, NOW.

The Jailer came trembling to Silas and Paul,
For a terror of darkness upon him did fall;—
"How *can* I be saved ? unto whom shall I bow ?
Who will hear my sad cry, and deliver me now ?"

Now, now ! lost one, now !
It is Jesus who died for thee ; trust in him now !

" 'Tis only believe in thy Saviour and Lord ;
And Salvation receive on the strength of his word ! "
The Jailer believed, and his name did avow,
Who hath rescued poor sinners, and rescues them
     now !

   Cho :

They ate and they drank in the joy of the Lord ;
And the joy reached to heaven, for the lost one
     restored ;—
And, seated in glory, a crown on his brow,
Is the Jailer, once urged to " Believe on him now ! "

   Cho :

                                             Acts 16.

THE GLAD NEWS.

A CORINTHIAN SONG.

O what a blessing the Gospel has come,
Over the sea to our city and home!
Worshipping idols, and sunken in sin,
Sad was our state till the Gospel came in!

O, it was sweet to hear the glad news!—
Hear the glad news—tell the glad news!
O, it was sweet to hear the glad news—
"Jesus has died for me!"

Jesus told Paul in the visions of night,
Never to cease, but to preach with his might;—
Many there were, in the city abroad,
Still to be brought, reconciled, unto God!

Cho:

So in our houses, and so in the street,
Ever with sinners we talk as we meet;—
Showing them all how Salvation is free—
Saying to each, "It was Jesus saved *me!*"

Cho:

Acts 18: 4-11.

SAUL OF TARSUS.

As many as my sins have been,
  So many let my praises be,
To him whose door I entered in,
  And found relief from misery.

I saw my Saviour on my way,
  And then I knew my soul he prized;
And to my longest, latest day
  I'll preach the Name I once despised!

O, men may cast his love away,
  And scorn a safety bought with blood:
But I'll maintain—reject who may—
  That Jesus is the Christ of God!

And in that Name, and by that love,
  I'll patient bear my weary way;
Until my toils shall end above
  With Jesus, in Eternal day!

Acts 22

THOU MUST KEEP ME!

Thou must keep me, O my Father!
   Keep and save thy trusting child!
Fierce the foes that round me gather,—
   All my prospect dark and wild.
Keep me ever! keep me ever!
   Thou, my God, art reconciled!

Make me daring in the danger;
   'Tis to try thy children's faith;—
Sloth and slumber is a stranger
   To the Trust that smiles at death!
Lord, I'll trust thee; Lord, I'll trust thee!
   Trust thee to my latest breath!

'Tis not I they'd slay and slander;—
   'Tis not I alone, abhorred;—
Gladly would their hatred wander
   From the Saint, to smite his Lord!
Save me, Jesus! Save me, Jesus!
   I have nothing but thy word!

Chains and prisons for Christ's hero;
   Praise and power for Sin and Wrong!
All the Earth against thy children—
   Son of God, how long? how long?
Break the bondage! Break the bondage!
   Let the world know thou art strong!

Acts xxiii. 1-10.

HALF PERSUADED.

Half persuaded to believe him ;
  Half in love with heavenly **truth** ;—
Half persuaded to receive him—
  Friend **of age,** and Guide of youth !

*   O believe him ! O receive him !*
*   Wait not for another day !*
*   You he calls from Earth to Heaven ;*
*   Hearken, Sinner ; come away !*

One there **was,** almost persuaded,
  Yet he gained no heavenly **crown.**
Wavering will, emotion faded,
  Never brought a blessing down.

    Cho. :

Well-persuaded, help obtaining—
  See the Christian firmly stand !
Joyfully the truth maintaining—
  Waiting for the Heavenly Land !
                    Acts xxvi. 28

A SCOTCH PARAPHRASE.

My heart it is weary and waitin',
   I'm ready, fu' ready to gae;
Like the birdie that hears i' the dawin',
   The voice o' the South, "Come away!"
I hae foughen the fecht o' the Righteous,
   I hae run i' the race o' the Just;
And aye to the end o' the battle
   I hae keepit my tryst and my trust!

Henceforth a' the mirk is ahint me—
   Before me it's glory I see;
And the crown o' the humble and holy
   The Lord has been keepin' for me.
O dochter and son! are ye faithfu'?
   Are ye rinnin' the race that I ran?
Are ye keepin' your ee on the Saviour,
   The friend and the fellow o' man?

For high in his holiness waitin',
   The Lord has a crown for to gie
To ilka puir sair-fittit rinner
   That comes a' forfoughten like me.
And wha has an ee for his comin',
   Lookin' up frae the strife and the stoure,
Shall himsel' see the King in his beauty,
   When the din o' the battle is ower!

                    2 Tim. iv. 6-8.

I HEAR THE WORD.

I hear the word, the welcome word,
That tells me of a loving Lord ;
And points the path the Sinner flies
To claim his perfect Sacrifice !
But *hearing* only, could not save,
Until my heart to God I gave !—
The Father calls the wanderers home,
But only they are saved who come !

To do thy will let it be mine,—
An aim how blessed and divine !
Not only be a *hearer* still,
But *doer* of thy perfect will !
Not one who catches in a glass,
Dim, fleeting figures, as they pass,—
But gazing, till my soul shall be
Changed to his image, whom I see !

For all that's good, and all that's true—
The heart to feel, the heart to do—
Are from the Father's hand above,
The Great unchanging Light of Love !
Then let me, with all meekness, learn
To good incline, from ill to turn ;—
Remembering, if like Christ I be,
Christ will not turn away from me !

James i. 1-16, 17.

THE WALLS OF HEAVEN ARE HIGH.

The walls of Heaven are high,
   Its towers are bright and fair,
Yet o'er that mount my thoughts can fly,
   To meet my Saviour there!

The gates of Heaven are strong,
   No foe can thither come;
Yet wide they open to the throng
   Of pilgrims marching home!

The air of Heaven is balm,
   And fadeless are its flowers;—
I reach toward that perfect calm,
   And breathe amidst its bowers!

The King of Heaven is high
   Lord over land and sea;
And yet I walk beneath his eye,
   And know he thinks of me!

The light of Heaven is God;
   A sun and shield for aye;
And beams of glory light the road
   That lights me on to Day!

The day of Heaven draws near,
   The day of Earth wears past;
O Thou who hast received me here,
   Receive me there at last!

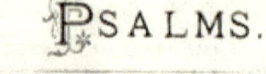

Psalms.

"Sing us one of the songs of Zion."
—Ps. 137.

Psalms.

I have, at occasional moments, during a long course of years, employed myself on the Psalms. I find, by looking over my papers, that only fifteen now remain, to complete the whole. I give here a selection of the shortest and best-rendered ones.—W. W. S.

THE GODLY.

PSALM I.

HAPPY he, who day by day
    Avoids the wicked race;—
Is never found in sinners' way,
    Nor in the scorner's place!

But in the statutes of the Lord
    Finds ever fresh delight;
And in the counsels of his word
    Delights him day and night.

Like a fair tree that strikes its root
    Beside the river's wave,—
God's grace shall perfect all his fruit,—
    His leaf unfading save.

How far diverse, in life and death,
    The haters of the Lord !
They fly as chaff before his breath,
    When judgment whets the sword !

For wants and ways of all his own
    Will he in love provide :
But sinners' ways are overthrown,
    And wrath pursues their pride !

THE COMING OF THE KING.

PSALM II.

Let heathen rage, and kings combine—
    But Jesus reigneth still ;
"O let us break his bands," they say,
" And cast his cords from us away !"
Yet shall he reign to endless day ;—
    His throne is Zion's hill.
The King has come to Zion's throne ;
The Lord's Anointed reigns alone !

Our God declares the firm decree,—
    " My Son this day, art Thou !
O ask, and I shall give to thee
The utmost land by every sea ;

And glory of the earth shall be
  A crown upon the brow !
The King has come to Zion's throne ;
The Lord's Anointed reigns alone !

Thou, Christ, shall rule with rod of power ;
  Thy might, with awe we see ;—
We kiss the hand that saves from woe,
And follow where thy footsteps go ; —
O blessed are the saints below,
  Who put their trust in thee !
The King has come to Zion's throne ;
The Lord's Anointed reigns alone !

THE FAITHFUL FRIEND.

PSALM XII.

Help, Lord ! the godly cease,
  And faith itself decays ;
Each to his neighbor whispering peace,
  With double, flattering ways.

The Lord shall cast away
  All those that speak in pride ;
" We are our own ! " they falsely say,
  " And who is lord beside ? "

In thee the poor, oppressed,
    And needy, full of sighs,
Shall safety find, O Lord, and rest
    From those that round them rise.

Thy words shall ever last,
    Holy, and pure and tried ;
As silver in the furnace cast,
    And seven times purified.

Thou shalt thy people hide,
    In this most evil hour ;
For wicked walk on every side
    When evil men have power !

THE CREATOR'S POWER.

PSALM XXIX.

Give to the Lord alone,
    Angel and mighty one—
Give to Jehovah all glory and might !
    Render him majesty,
    Worship and praise in thee—
Beauty of Holiness ! Courts of Delight

God's mighty voice is known
Waters and floods upon ;—
Thunders Jehovah in glory abroad ;—
On the great floods he rides,
Strength in his words abides,—
Greatness and majesty wait upon God !

Breaketh the voice of God
Trees from their high abode,—
Cedars of strength, even Lebanon, thine !
Bending thy forests down,
Lebanon ! Sirion !
Leaping and skipping like calves of the kine.

Lightnings and flaming fire,
Glancing and cleft expire,
At the dread voice of God sounding below ;—
Trembles the wilderness,
Quaking in sore distress—
Kadesh is shaken, and reels to and fro.

Beasts of the wilderness
Terror and pain oppress ;
Bared are the forests that stood in their pride ;
While in his presence bow
Angels and men below,
Singing his glory in whom they abide.

Floods are his royal seat,
Earth is beneath his feet,—

Throned o'er the universe sits he forever !
 All who may seek his face,
 Strength shall receive, and grace ;
God wiil his people still blesss and deliver !

CONFESSION AND PARDON.

PSALM XXXII.

Blessed he, for evermore,
 Whose transgression is removed !
He whose sin is covered o'er
 By the Saviour he hath loved !
Joy that yieldeth heavenly fruits
 Dwells with him to whom the Lord
No iniquity imputes—
 Guileless resting on his word.

Silence o'er my sin I kept,
 While my bones and frame decayed ;
All the day I mourned and wept,
 Vainly seeking human aid.
Day and night thy chastening hand
 Heavy on my spirit lay,—
Till my soul was like a land
 Parched beneath the Summer's ray.

To the Lord, in my distress,
   I acknowledged all my sin ;
My transgressions to confess
   Did my troubled heart begin.
Thou forgavest, in thy grace,
   All the guilt of every sin !
When I humbly sought thy face,
   Thou didst let the wanderer in !

Thus shall all the godly race
   Ever in thy love abound—
Supplicate thy throne of grace,—
   Seek thee where thou may'st be found !
Surely in the whelming flood,
   Threatening dire destruction round,
They who calmly rest on God
   Have a blest deliverance found !

Thou my hiding-place shalt be ;
   And from trouble safely guide ;
All my songs shall be of thee—
   Hedged with joy on every side.
Lo, saith God, I will thee teach
   In the way thy feet should try ;
Whersoe'er thy journeys reach,
   I will guide thee with mine eye !

Be not as the unreasoning horse,
   Or the mule within the field,—
Brought within thy reach by force,—
   Lord, instruct us how to yield !

Sorrows to the wicked come,—
    Mercy round the child of grace ;—
Sing, ye righteous ! travelling home ;
    Shout for joy, ye upright race !

FOLLOWING HARD.

PSALM XLII.

As pants the hart for water brooks,
    Pursued afar, and sorely pressed,—
So pants my soul, and upward looks
    To thee for rest !

For thee I thirst, O God, alone ;
    For thee, the living God, for thee !
When shall I come before thy throne,
    My God to see ?

My tears have been my meat by day ;
    My sighs the night-wind bears abroad ;
As came my mocking foes to say
    " Where is thy God ?"

This I remember, and lament,
    And pour my soul in sighs to thee ;—
For once I with thy people went,
    Thy Courts to see :—

With solemn joy they onward swept,
   The Lord in his own house to praise ;
And with the multitude I kept
     God's holy-days.

Then why art thou cast down, my soul ?
   Dejected, and to grief a prey ;—
Hope thou in God ! his smile shall roll
     Thy gloom away !

Cast down, my God, and sorely tried,
   My soul to thee turns yearning still ;
From Jordan's land, and Hermon's side,
     And Mizar's hill.

Afar, deep calleth unto deep,
   Thy waterspouts I hear with dread :
Thy waters close, thy billows leap,
     Above my head !

The Lord to me will yet display
   His love, and calm my spirit's strife ;—
My song by night, my prayer by day—
     God of my life !

I'll say unto the Lord, my Rock,
   " Why hast thou me forgotten so ?"
For foes oppress, and haters mock,
     And I have woe !

My foes' reproach, within each bone,
    Is daily like a piercing sword ;
They say, " Where is thy Refuge flown ?
    And where's thy Lord ?"

But why, my soul, art thou cast down ?
    Disquieted in sore amaze ?
Trust him who is my health, my crown,
    My God ! my Praise !

THE CITY OF THE GREAT KING.

PSALM XLVIII.

Jehovah is great ! be his praises the same
In the hearts of the people he calls by his name ;—
The city wherein is his earthly abode—
The mount of his holiness—chosen of God.

How beautiful Zion, the joy of the Earth !
How lovely her place, on the sides of the North !
The city where reigneth the Great King of kings,
In her palaces known by the blessings he brings !

Lo, kings were assembled in battle array,—
They saw it, they marvelled, and hasted away !
For fear fell upon them, with trembling and dread,—
They came in their might, but all fainting they fled !

The ships of the Islands lie broken abroad :
As we heard, we have seen in the City of God,
How God will in Zion his glory display,
Establish her peace, and protect her for aye.

We have thought of thy goodness, and paid thee our
    vows,
O God, our own God ! in the midst of thine house ;
As great as thy name shall thy praise ever be,
And thy right hand with righteousness laden we see.

O Zion rejoice ! in thy God ever blest !
Ye daughters of Judah, how sweet may ye rest !
And in gladness of spirit exult in your God,
Because of his judgments and glory abroad.

Go walk about Zion, and tell ye her towers ;—
How strong are her bulwarks ! how peaceful her
    bowers !
Her palaces mark, where in safety we dwell—
That ye to your children the story may tell !

For this mighty God is our God and our Friend,
For ever and ever, and world without end ;—
He'll never forsake us, our journey beneath,
But guide us and comfort us, even to death.

"MY HEART IS FIXED."

PSALM LVII.

Be merciful to me, O God !
  Be merciful to me !
No more a wanderer far abroad
  My spirit flies to thee !
Beneath the shadow of thy wings,
My soul in peace and safety sings,
Till past are these distressings things ;
  Be merciful to me !

O God, I cry to thee, most high !
  To God, and shall prevail ;
Who doth perform for me, when I
  In mine own strength should fail.
He sends from Heaven in danger's hour,
And saves from foes who would devour ;
And shall his truth and mercy pour ;—
  O God, I cry to thee !

My soul is sore distressed, among
  The lions of the earth ;—
I make my bed where guilt and wrong
  Like fire is breaking forth :
E'en sons of men whose gnashing teeth
Are spears and arrows set for death ;
A sword their tongue, and fire their breath
  My soul is sore distressed !

Be thou exalted high, O God,
　　Above the Heavens of light!
And let thy glory shine abroad
　　O'er Earth's sublimest height!
A net they for my steps prepared—
And while my soul of help despaired,
In pits they digged themselves are snared:
　　Be thou exalted high!

My heart is fixed! O God, my heart
　　Is set upon thy praise!
With voice of psalm, and tuneful art,
　　I'll bless thee all my days!
Awake, my heart! awake, my tongue!
Awake, my psaltery and my song!
With harp I'll join the early throng—
　　My heart is fixed, O God!

I'll praise thee, O my God, among
　　All people of the earth;
And show thy praise with joyful tongue
　　To every nation forth!
For high as Heaven thy mercies are,—
Thy truth, not height of clouds declare,—
O'er heaven and earth exalted far!
　　I'll praise thee, O my God!

THE SHELTERING ROCK.

PSALM LXI.

O hear me, Jehovah ! attend to my prayer :
    From ends of the earth unto thee will I cry ;—
When my heart is o'erburdened with sorrow and care,
    O lead to the Rock that is higher than I !

My shade and my shelter thou ever hast been !
    My tower of defence that security brings ;—
Let me dwell in the Courts where thy glory is seen,
    And trust evermore in the shade of thy wings !

O God, thou hast heard and accepted my vow,
    And giv'st me a portion with those that are thine ;
Thou wilt lengthen the life of thy servant below,
    And establish his throne in Emmanuel's line.

He ever doth sit before God as a king,
    And thy mercy and truth shall surround him for aye ;
For this unto thee endless praise will I sing,
    And daily thy vows to thy name will I pay !

CHRIST'S DOMINION.

PSALM LXXII.

Give the king thy judgments, Lord !
Give thy grace unto the Son !
He shall righteously award
Judgment for the poor, thine own.
Mountains now his peace shall speak,
And the hills his judgments show ;—
He shall judge the poor and meek—
Lay the proud oppressors low.

Far from sea to sea extends
His dominion, breaking forth ;
From the river to the ends
Of the renovated earth.
Desert tribes shall now draw near,
Bending low before his throne ;—
All his enemies in fear
Low in dust his power shall own.

Corn, a handful in the earth,
On the barren mountains sown,
Now shall bring a harvest forth—
Soon shall shake like Lebanon !
They that of Mount Zion are,
City of the living God—
O'er the earth shall bloom afar,—
Bear his glory far abroad.

Ever shall his name endure,
Far and wide his glory run;
Still continued, firm and sure,—
Changeless, lasting, as the sun.
And in him shall blessed be
Men of every tribe and tongue,—
Nations all, his glory see—
Call him blessed in their song.

THE COURTS OF THE LORD.

PSALM LXXXIV.

Lord of Hosts, how loved and fair
All thy tabernacles are!
Longs my soul to nestle there,
Fainting for thy Courts afar.
Heart and flesh cry out for thee—
For thy glory and thy grace;—
O the living God to see
In his blessed dwelling-place!

E'en the sparrow broods among
Hallowed scenes of peace and prayer;
And the swallow with her young
Near thine altars may repair.

Lord of Hosts, my God and King!
Happy they who dwell with thee!
In thy house with joy to sing
Praise to thee continually.

Lord of Hosts, and Jacob's God!
Hear our prayer as thus we bow!
Look, O God our shield, abroad,
See thine own Anointed now!
Better than a thousand more,
One day spent thy Courts within;
I had rather keep thy door,
Than to dwell in tents of sin!

Sun and shield our God shall be,—
Grace and glory will he give;
No good thing withhold will he
From the men who upright live.
O Jehovah! God of Hosts!
Blessed ever shall he be,
Who, despising other boasts,
Trusts his soul, his all, on thee!

THE CITY OF OUR GOD.

PSALM LXXXVII.

In the mountains his foundation
    Firm and sure shall e'er abide;
God the gates of our salvation
    Loveth more than all beside
Glorious things are spoken ever,
    O thou city of our God,—
Of thy gifts, and of their Giver,
    Of thy Saints, and their abode!

God shall speak of Egypt, Babel,
    As of those that know his name;
Gentile nations all enable
    To behold him through the Lamb.
Sons from far shall sound his praises,
    And of Zion shall be told
How her God each bulwark raises,—
    Who was born within her fold.

God himself shall write in glory,
    Where the names of Saints appear,
To the praise of Zion's story,
    " These were born and nurtured there!"
Harps and songs of exultation
    Shall thy children's welcome be;
City of the Saints' salvation,
    All my springs are found in thee!

OUR ALMIGHTY FRIEND.

PSALM XCV.

Come, and let us sing to God,—
   Joyful noises sweetly blending;
Our salvation's Rock abroad
   Sound in praises never ending!
Come we then before his face,
Come with love, and come with grace;
With thanksgiving sweetly blending
Psalms and praises never ending.

For the Lord is God on high,
   King above all gods forever;
In his hands Earth's caverns lie,
   Towering hills are in his quiver.
His the sea, and his the land,
Formed beneath his mighty hand,—
Isle and shore, and mount and river—
King above all gods forever!

Come, and let us worship now,
   Bending down before him lowly;
Humbly seek with prayer and vow,
   God our Maker, blest and holy.
He our God, to bless and keep,—
He our Shepherd, we his sheep—
On his hand all waiting lowly;
He forever blest and holy!

If to-day his voice ye hear,
    Let no hearts be unbelieving,—
As when once in desert drear
    God was o'er your fathers grieving.
" Forty years," saith God, " with grief
Bore I with their unbelief ;
Till I sware, This race backsliding,
In my Rest hath no abiding !"

EXALTED PRAISE.

PSALM CXIII.

Praise the Lord in accents fervent !
Praise his name, each happy servant !
Praise the Lord the glorious Giver—
Blessed now, and blest forever !

From the sunrise, onward flying,
To the sunset-glory, dying,
Praise him, high o'er every nation—
Glorious in his own creation !

Who like God ? whose praises swelling,
Sound through Heaven, his glorious dwelling :
Yet whose love becomes so lowly
Heaven to view, and men unholy.

From the dust the poor God raises;
Now a prince, he claims his praises;—
Blessings cheer the lonely dwelling—
Praise him, all his love forthtelling!

A PLAINT.

PSALM CXX.

When my soul was low, I cried
Unto God who was my Guide;
And he heard me, when his hearing was my peace!
O deliver thou my soul,
Out of lying lips' control;—
From deceitful tongues, whose slanders do not cease.

What shall come to thee, O tongue,
Full of falsehood and of wrong?
Sharp arrows of the mighty, burning coals:—
Woe is me in Mesech dwelling!
And in tents of Kedar telling
All the sorrows that surround afflicted souls!

For, too long my soul hath dwelt
With the men who falsely dealt
With my Saviour, and would falsely deal with me; -
For I plead for love and peace,
And that war and strife may cease,—
But they shout against my soul, O God! and thee!

THE CITY OF GOD.

PSALM CXXII.

O how glad my soul and spirit,
   When with joy they said to me,
"Let us, who his love inherit,
   Go, his dwelling-place to see!"
In thy courts our feet with gladness
   Yet shall stand, Jerusalem!
Weary feet, and hearts of sadness,
   Thy strong gates shall shelter them!

Built, and planned, and walled together,
   One the city, one the aim;—
All the tribes, ascending thither,
   Praise and bless Jehovah's name.
There are set the thrones, redressing
   Wrong and ill, ev'n David's throne:—
Pray ye for Jerusalem's blessing;
   In her peace shall be your own!

Peace within thy walls be ever!
   Joy in every palace shine!
For the sake of loved companions,
   Still my prayer is, "Peace be thine!"
For the House of God within thee—
   In mine eyes Earth's brightest gem—
Every blessing I would win thee,
   My sweet home, Jerusalem!

AID IMPLORED.

PSALM CXXIII.

To thee I lift mine eyes, O God !
Who hast in Heaven thy blest abode !
As servants near the master stand,
To watch the waving of his hand—
Or meek-eyed maids, with looks sedate,
Obedient on their mistress wait,—
So wait our eyes, O God, on thee,
Till we thy grace and glory see.

O **Lord,** show mercy unto us !
Thy loving-kindness reach us thus :
For with contempt our souls they fill—
Contempt of those who seek our ill.
Our souls are whelmed beneath **the scorn**
Of those to ease and luxury born ;—
Filled with contempt, the scorn of pride—
In thee alone our souls confide !

AN ANTHEM.

PSALM CXXIV.

If it had not been the Lord
    Who appeared upon our side —
If it had not been the Lord,
    With the battle raging wide —
We alive had soon gone down,—
    Soul, and faith, and hope o'erthrown,
When the foemen closed around us in their might ; —
    Then had waters whelmed us o'er,
    Like a flood on fertile shore,
And in ruin we had sunken from the sight !

    But now blessed be the Lord,
        Who hath saved us from a prey !
    Like a trembling, hunted bird,
        From the snare escaped away :
    So our soul is now set free,
    And our praises rise to thee,
Who art Helper of the helpless, evermore !
    For thy name, Almighty Lord,
    Is our panoply and guard !—
And with Heaven and Earth our Maker we adore !

GOD'S PROTECTION.

PSALM CXXV.

O safe they stand who trust to thee,
    With life-long, fond endeavour!
They stand as stands the Hill of God,
    Forever and forever!

As round about the sacred fane
    The guardian mountains gather,
Ev'n so the Lord is round his Saints—
    The ever-blessed Father!

The Righteous shall enjoy their lot,—
    No wicked dispossessing;
But thou shalt keep their hands from sin,
    And build them with thy blessing.

O let thy favour fall on those
    Who would be pure and holy!
And bless the men of upright hearts,
    The loving and the lowly!

For those that turn aside to sin
    To darkest doom are driven;
But peace shall rest on Israel,—
    The peace that falls from Heaven!

OUT OF CAPTIVITY.

PSALM CXXVI.

It was like a dream of gladness,
Breaking on a night of sadness,
When the Lord, to Zion turning,
   Bade her weary wanderers come ;—
Then our mouth was filled with singing,
And with joy the valleys ringing,
Made the very heathen wonder
   At the bliss that brought us home !

For great things the Lord did for us ;
And we joined the joyful chorus,
"Thou wilt turn us, and refresh us,
   Like the desert-streams in rain !"
Tearful sowing has glad reaping—
Precious seed, borne forth in weeping,
Shall, by God the Spirit's blessing,
   Bring the golden sheaves again !

THE BLESSING OF THE SAINT.

PSALM CXXVII.

Only as God builds the house strong and deep,
   Their labors are bless'd who are building and toiling ;
Only as God the city doth keep,
   Safety and peace o'er the portals are smiling !

Vain to rise up, and midnight to keep ;
   Vain to eat bread of labor and sorrow ;
For so his beloved he giveth his sleep,
   A calm brooding night, and a blessed to-morrow.

Sons of the righteous, and children of grace—
   A heritage blest to the godly forever ;—
These stand in the battle, with sin face to face,
   Like a warrior stern with a well-filled quiver.

Happy the man with such weapons in hand—
   A righteous seed, in his footsteps pursuing ;—
Honored and blest among men shall he stand ;
   Enemies never shall work his undoing !

SUFFERING.

PSALM CXXIX.

O many a time, and many a way,
    From youth my foes afflicted me;—
Yea, often thus, may Israel say,
    Yet victory shall they never see!

The plowers plowed upon my back—
    Is that my Saviour that I see?
The lash made long its furrowed track—
    Ah Lord! and it was borne for me!

Our God is righteous, and in wrath
    Hath cut asunder every cord
Of sin; and turned them in their path,
    Who hate the Zion of the Lord.

Like withering grass on housetop found,
    So shall the wicked fade away;
Nor blessings from the Lord abound,
    For which his children wait and pray.

OUT OF THE DEPTHS.

PSALM CXXX.

Out of the depths, weary and sad,
 Out of the depths I cry to thee!
Lord, hear my voice, and make me glad,
 And let thine ear attentive be!

Lord, if thou stood'st, sin to reprove,
 Who should escape? and who should stand?
But there's forgiveness in thy love,
 That we may fear, and bless thy hand.

Wait for the Lord! Soul, do thou wait!
 Only on his sweet word I stay:
Yea, like the watch that keep the gate,
 And hail the dawning of the day.

Israel's hope ever shall rest
 Only in God, who mercy shows;—
With full redemption ever bless'd
 From all our sins, and all our woes!

HUMILITY.

PSALM CXXXI.

My heart is not haughty, my heart is with thee ;
Mine eyes are not lofty, no sin would I see ;—
In things that are mighty, and things that are high,
I keep myself humble, as lowly I lie.

And walking thus meekly and humbly a child,
As babe of its mother bereft and beguiled,
My hope, with all Israel, still is the Lord ;
And ever and ever we'll trust in his word !

LOVE OF BRETHREN.

PSALM CXXXIII.

How good, and how happy, and pleasant it is,
   For brethren to dwell united together !
Like ointment all precious, the blessing is his,
   Who dwells in the fragrance that Peace brings with
      her!

Like ointment all holy, that fragrantly fell
   The Priest and his raiment to bless and to hallow,
Like the dew, with a blessing, all silent and still,
   On Hermon descending, o'er fields parched and yellow;

Thus love among brethren : 'tis pure as the dew
  The mountains of Zion in beauty restoring—
All lovely and blest for Jehovah to view ;
  For ever and ever his blessing outpouring.

BLESSING.

PSALM CXXXIV.

Ye stars, that through the silent night
  Your torches lift for God—
Who stand, obedient in his sight,
  And wait upon his nod ;—
And all your hands, ye earthly throng,
  Lift up with glad acclaim,
And bless the Lord, his Courts among,
  For holy is his name !

The Lord that made the heaven and earth,
  The Lord that made the skies—
The God that shines in Zion forth,
  And bids our hope arise—
Yea, he who saves us from all ill,
  His blessing send thee now,
And balm that breathes from Zion's hill
  Descend upon thy brow !

THE EXILES' LAMENT.

PSALM CXXXVII.

By the rivers of Babylon sadly we wept,
    As we thought of returning to Zion no more ;
And the harps of our gladness all silently slept
    On the boughs of the willows that wept on the shore !

For heartless they came, who had borne us afar,
    And their mandate was, " Mirth, and melodious lays !"
And they who had spoiled us with ravage and war,
    Cried, "Sing us a song in Jerusalem's praise !"

But how shall we sing in the aliens' land,
    The songs that Jehovah once hearkened to hear ?
O Zion, let perish my ready right hand,
    If fades from my bosom thine image so dear !

Thou home of my heart, if I cherish not thee,
    Let my tongue sink in silence, my gladness be o'er,
If high o'er all treasures, possessed or to be,
    I place not Jerusalem, blest evermore !

On Edom and Babylon terrors shall fall,
    Who mocked when Jerusalem's woes followed fast ;
For ever the same that they measured withal,
    Shall be the return the Lord gives them at last !

THE EVER-PRESENT GOD.

PSALM CXXXIX.

O Lord, thou hast searched me and known me,
    My coming and going are thine!
Thou knowest each thought and endeavour;
    My guide and my guard is divine!

No word I can say or imagine
    But thou understandest it well;
Thy hand is upon me to guide me—
    Such wisdom I fail to forthtell?

O where could I go from thy Spirit?
    Or where could I flee from thy sight?
If I rise up to Heaven, 'tis thy presence!
    And the darkness of death is all light!

If wafted on wings of the morning
    Away to the uttermost sea,—
Even there shall my Saviour sustain me;
    His hand and his heart are with me!

If I cling to the cover of darkness,
    The night shall betray me in light;—
Alike to thine infinite knowledge:
    No sin can be hidden in night.

How precious, O God, is each promise,
    How loving each thought unto me!
In life I shall live in thy favor;
    And awaking, shall still be with thee!

O search me, my Father! and know me;—
    My thoughts and my heart are with thee!
Take away every wicked emotion,
    And lead me thy glory to see!

UNIVERSAL PRAISE.

PSALM CXLVIII.

Praise the Lord; from Heaven praise him!
    Praise him in the highest height!
Praise him all ye Angels, praise him!
    Sun and moon, and stars of light!
Praise him all ye heaven of heavens;—
    Watery worlds above our gaze—
Praise the Lord, who hath commanded
    And creates you for his praise.

He the floods hath set forever—
    Bound them by Divine decree:—
Praise the Lord, the glorious Giver!
    Earth, and creatures of the sea.

Fire, and hail, and snow and vapor,—
  Stormy wind that works his will,—
Fruitful tree and towering cedar—
  Mountain rude, and rolling hill!

Praise him, beasts that wildly wander—
  Gentle herds in human care—
Creeping things, a countless number—
  Flying fowl that fill the air!
Praise him, kings and princes praise him!
  All ye people, join in one ;—
Let the rulers bow before him,
  Youth and maiden, sire and son!

Let them sing his praise forever,—
  For his name alone is great ;—
High above the Earth and Heaven
  Is his glory and his state!
Power he giveth to his people—
  Praise he doth his saints afford ;
E'en to Israel, ever near him—
  Praise, all people, praise the Lord!

ECSTATIC PRAISE.

PSALM CVIII.

O God, my heart is fixed ;
   Thy praise my tongue shall keep !
Wake, harp and psaltry again !
And I myself to join the strain
   Will early wake from sleep.

I'll praise thee, O my God ;
   Among all people praise !
For high as Heaven thy mercies rise ;
And far above these lower skies
   Thy truth its light displays.

Be thou exalted, Lord,
   Above the heavens we see ;—
O'er all the earth thy glory beam,
Thy well-beloved to redeem—
   O save and answer me !

From trouble give release !
   For human help is vain ;—
Through God shall we do valiantly,
For he our helper still shall be,
   And tread our foes amain.

"Sing me a bairn's hymn."

—Dr. Guthrie, on his death-bed.

Children's Pieces.

THE PRINCE AND THE BEGGAR.

A POOR man sat outside the gate
    Of the Beautiful City (Heaven its name!)
And he wished, he wished he could enter in;
But well he knew he was covered with sin,—
    And there he sat, waiting the same.

But the Prince in royal robes went by,
    And he looked on the man all covered with sin;—
"Would you like to come in? Would you like to dwell
    In the Beautiful City, so holy and fair?"   [there?
        "Oh, Prince! I can never come in!"

"Nay, nay, my poor friend, there's love for thee!"
    ('Twas Jesus who spoke, and he knew his voice;)
"Come dwell in my palace, and be my friend;
    And service and love, without measure or end,
        Shall make thy poor heart rejoice!"

So the Prince and the Beggar went arm in arm,
    And the gates wide opened to give them way;—
And I thought, "Since Jesus came here to save,
And for my great sins his dear life gave—
    I'll go with him now to-day!"

WHEN OUR SHIP COMES IN.

I know a little maiden,
   That lives within the wood ;
As cheerful as a little bird,
   As happy and as good.—
There's many a thing that she might have
   She ne'er can hope to win ;
She laughs, and says she'll have it,
   " When her ship comes in !"

When our ship comes in !
When our ship comes in !
What gold we all shall gather
When our ship comes in !

And servants to obey her,
   She makes my dog and cat ;
And gathers up her pinafore,
   And asks, " What silk is *that ?*"
And as she sups her bread and milk
   Says, holding up her tin,
She'll have a golden platter
   When her ship comes in !

   Cho :

Ah, happy little maiden !
   To us with message sent,

To let vain wishes go, and keep
The measureless content!
Whate'er our Father gives, shall meet
With gratitude within;
And for the rest—we'll have it
When our ship comes in!
Cho:

GATHER THE FLOWERS.

Gather the flower that hidden lies
  Deep in the dew like a truant gem;
Gather the buds that stately rise—
  Two of a color, and three on a stem:
    "Yes," said my child, "I'll gather them well;
    For which is the sweetest I cannot tell!"

Gather the flowers that speak of hope,
  Scenting the breath of the morning hour;
Gather the buds that only ope
  When night comes apace, and tempests lower!
    "Yes," said my sweet one, "for both are bright;
    One's for the morning, the other for night."

"And is it not strange," she gently said,
  As she laid down beside me the spoils that were ours,
"That since I loved Jesus, so oft I've been led
  To thank him for Summer, and sunshine and flowers!
    It seems as if *now* I'm but learning to look
    On the woods and the fields as a leaf of God's book!"

WONDROUS STAR.

A star is in the western sky ;—
   How lovely is its light !
And with its glory-beaming eye
   It sets not all the night !
I must away, I cannot stay,
   It leads me from afar !
I follow thee by night and day,
   O bright and wondrous Star !

I found the blessed Lord had come,
   To save a world of woe ;
A babe within a humble home,
   Yet King of all below.
With love untold I gave him gold,
   And gifts I brought from far,—
As o'er my soul thy glory rolled,
   Salvation's risen star !

Nor from the East or West alone,
   Shall hearts be led to thee ;
But they shall come, thy name to own,
   From every land and sea.
O brightly rise, and let our eyes
   Behold thee from afar—
The Truth that makes the nations wise,
   The Bright and Morning Star !

                  —Matt. ii. 2.

THE TEN COMMANDMENTS.

One God, one only; our Father good and kind;—
Images to worship, will lead away the mind.
God's name so holy O do thou still revere,
And a blessing find in the Sabbath dear!

Love father, mother, so watchful, true and kind;
Let not hate nor murder once enter to thy mind;—
Blest loving Father, O still thy Spirit give,
That our sinful souls may look up and live!

No vileness tempt thee, in thought, or word or deed;—
Honest be, and truthful; nor covet in thy need.
Love ever truly, with all thy heart and mind,
God, the blessed God, who is ever kind!

—Ex. xx. 1-21.

THE VISITOR.

Bonnie, bonnie bairnie, whither didst thou come?
From the Land ayont the Sky, to find another home!

Bonnie, bonnie bairnie, what wert thou doing there?
Lying 'mang the lily-bells, and growing guid and fair!

Bonnie, bonnie bairnie, how didst thou think of this?
God saw the bairn-love in thy heart, and told me with a
    kiss!

Bonnie, bonnie bairnie, and wilt thou bide for aye?
I'll bide until the blythe bidding, that gars me hie away!

Bonnie, bonnie bairnie, and shall I now find rest?
Thy rest is where I gat this smile—upon the Father's
    breast!

SEEING NOT, YET LOVING.

  "Now what did Jesus look like?"
    Said my sweet child to me;
  "I like to picture to myself
    The friends I cannot see:
But I have looked my Bible through,
    And find not in it all,
If his kind eyes were black or blue,
    Or he in person tall.

  "I know his voice was kindest,
    For Mary loved its tone;
I know his smile was sweetest,
    For it hushed each weary moan:—

But oft I wish I had been there,
    Myself to hear and see
How Jesus looked in Bethany,
    Or talked in Galilee!"

"No likeness now remains to us,
    My little one," said I,
"Of this, our dearest Friend on earth,
    Our dearest Friend on high!
'Twill blend our glory with surprise,
    When we to Heaven are brought,
That he should be ten thousand times
    Beyond our highest thought!

"EVEN A CUP OF COLD WATER."

"God be praised for sweet cold water!"
    Cries the pilgrim, as he sips
From the cup my little daughter
    Held up to his trembling lips;—
Tiptoe-standing, while he sate
    Close beside our wicket gate.

And she loves to drink that water,
    (Sweeter, since the pilgrim's need!)
And last Sabbath day I taught her
    That the Saviour loved the deed:
"Heaven-rewarded shall it be—
    For, done to those, 'tis done to *me!*"

IMPERFECT.

I come to the well, but its water
    Never quenches the thirsting within ;
I bathe in the sunlight of morning,
    When the hymns of creation begin—
But still there is something of sorrow,
    Because there is something of sin !

There is rapture, and gladness and glory,
    Around me in nature I see—
And my heart whispers sadly the story
    That the darkness and doubt is in me ;
That God and his works are all holy,
    And the sadness and sin is in me !

But I know that above there are blossoms,
    As fair as were Eden's at first ;
And the tree with the sweet leaves of healing,
    And waters for quenching of thirst ;—
And grief is forgot in the glory,
    And murmuring never rehearsed !

THE LINTIE.

'Twas in a peaceful English vale,
   Where the distant sea was gleaming—
Where the cuckoo sings and the daisy springs,
   And the sun through the sky is dreaming.

And a wee Scotch lass, blue-eyed, in tears,
   Beheld a skylark winging;
And his glad heart grew to her mystic view
   A spirit, gaily singing.

For she thought his home, like hers, was far
   'Mid the breckan and the heather;
In the rugged North, by the links of Forth,
   In that sweet April weather.

When, "Hey, my lass!" quoth an English man,
   "I've songsters for a treasure;
And as *Scotch* you are, in eyes and hair,
   Here's a Scotch bird for your pleasure!"

She saw the Scottish *lintie* there,
   His heart in exile pining;
And like twin stars, through the prison bars,
   His sad dark eyes were shining.

She had a sixpence ; 'twas her own,
    And it was all her treasure ;
Though sad and lone her heart had grown,
    She'd give the lintie pleasure !

She paid the price, she oped the door—
    On cottage thatch he lighted ;
He caught the sound of joy around,
    And poured his song, delighted.

Then stretched his wing for Northern skies,
    A liberated *linnet !*
And the lassie dear dried up each tear,
    For consolation in it !

And she found her exiled heart grew calm,
    And peace fell like a shadow,
When her heart was stirred to bless a *bird*,
    In that sweet English meadow !

O MY SAVIOUR.

Tune: "When He Cometh."

O my Saviour, tender hearted, cast o'er me thy mantle!
Let thy mercy, tender mercy, abide in my breast.
For thy voice is still pleading, in love interceding,
Saying, Bless thou thy brother as thou would'st be
    bless'd!

O my Saviour, let me judge not, lest it should condemn
    me!
For my soul is sorely stained if its worth should be
    proved!
And thy voice I hear pleading, in love interceding,
Saying, Love thou thy brother, as thou would'st be
    loved!

O my Saviour, I am nothing, yet great things I ask
    thee!
As thou givest I will give, for thy word I believe!
And thy voice is still pleading, in love interceding,
Saying, Give to thy brother as thou would'st receive!

BLESSED KINGDOM.

Far away, the Holy Spirit
   Points a promised Land on high,—
Flesh and blood can not inherit,
   And where sin comes never nigh!

Blessed Kingdom! Blessed Kingdom!
   Ours when Earth and toil are o'er:
At the sounding of the trumpet
   We shall change, to change no more!

Lo, the once victorious tyrant,
   Death himself shall conquered be!
Sin, the dart that smote the conscience,
   Has been slain at Calvary!

  Cho:

In immortal sinless beauty,
   All the saints of Christ shall rise:
O have courage! Brethren, faint not!
   Jesus calls you to the skies!

  Cho:

THE TONGUE.

A CHILDREN'S HYMN.

Lord, restrain a forward tongue,
   Busy with all else but thee ;
Lead me while my heart is young,
   Grace and holiness to see !

Let me speak like those above,
   Let me show thy grace abroad :—
On my tongue the law of love,
   In my heart the peace of God !

Waters from no fountain broad
   Sweet and bitter are conveyed ;
So the tongue that blesses God
   Must not curse whom God has made !

Cho :

Come thou Wisdom from above—
   Pure, and peaceable, and kind !
Now descending like a dove,
   Come and dwell within my mind !

Cho :

LITTLE WHITE-HEAD.

NURSERY RHYME.

Little White-Head rubs his eyes :
Little Black-Head thinks he'll rise ;
Little Red-Head's out at play—
Curly-Head be mine to-day !

Little White-Head—bread to eat ;
Little Black-Head—honey sweet ;
Little Red-Head drinks no wine—
Curly-Head is ever mine !

THE COW THAT RAN TO GODERICH.

NURSERY RHYME.

The cow that ran to Goderich
  To get a lick of salt,
Her name was gentle Bossy,
  And we told her of her fault !
She was so dry when she came home,
  She drank both night and day,
She would have drank Lake Huron,
  If they had let her stay !

TEN LITTLE FINGERS.

NURSERY RHYME.

Ten little fingers,
    Ten little toes;
One little chubby mouth,
    One round nose!
Two little ears,
    And one little head;
Now, my little boy,
    Time for bed!

Two little rosy cheeks,
    One little tongue,
Tired with prattling
    All day long!
Two little eyes,
    Like stars that peep;
Now, my little boy,
    Time for sleep!

DAVID AND JONATHAN.

How sweetly swelled the tide of love,
  'Twixt David's soul and Jonathan !
A streamlet from the fount above,
  That gathered glory as it ran.

I love to trace him as he went—
  That royal scion, brave and good ;
Leaving his father's kingly tent,
  To meet with David in the wood.

And though he knew that David's brow
  Should bear the crown instead of his,
His words were still, "The king be thou ;
  And I'll be near, where danger is !

"Thou shalt be King through Israel's coasts,
  By God appointed and preserved ;
And I'll be Captain of thy hosts,
  And serve thee as thou ne'er wast served !"

And so they made a covenant there,
  As brothers hand in hand they stood ;—
Then passed one on to noise and care,
  And one to silence in the wood.

SWEET TO KNOW.

Sweet to know our Heavenly Father
   Will to us no good deny;
He who gave his Son to save us,
   Shall with him all things supply.

Sweet to know he ever loves us;
   And poor sinners when they come,
Are conformed to Jesus' image—
   Marching to their heavenly home!

Sweet to know that nought shall sever
   From that loving Lord who came!
Death and hell and sin forever
   We have conquered through his name!

Sweet to know he waits to welcome
   Every soul that's sick of sin;—
He who stands before the Father
   Gives a blessed entrance in!

GLOSSARY

OF SCOTCH WORDS USED IN THE BOOK.

My Scotch readers will excuse my inserting this glossary. They don't need it; but others do: and there are many people, with a keen admiration and appreciation of Scottish literature, who are thankful for a little help over the hard places. And it is easy to make mistakes, as when the American took "gullie," in *Dr. Hornbook*, to mean a ravine, and thought Burns was threatening to throw his light-weight antagonist over a precipiece! I give the meaning of the words as they are found in the book: but there are often many other meanings to the words.

A.

A', all (prom. aw.)
Ae, ane, one.
Aboon, above.
Albyn, Scotland.
Ain, own.
Aiblins, perhaps.
Auld-farrant, old-fashioned.
Arena, are not.
Ayont, beyond.

B.

Bairn, child.
Belyre, by and bye.
Beek, bask.
Bent, short natural grass.
Big, build.
Biggit, built.
Birk, birken, birch.
Birr, resounding vigor.
Bield, shelter.
Blateness, bashfulness.
Blink, glance.
Blae, blue, pale.
Blythe, gay, cheerful.
Boo'd, bowed.
Bonnie, beautiful.
Brod, puncture.
Braw, gaudy.
Brattles, runs noisily.
Braird, tender sprout.
Branks, wooden bridle.
Braes, banks or hills.
Burn, a streamlet.
Breckans, ferns.
Busk, dress, adorn.

C.

Ca', call (pron. caw.)
Cairn, a pyramid of stones.
Cannie, gentle.
Cadger, beggar, "tramp."
Callant, boy.
Carritch, catechism.
Caller, fresh.
Caudron, caldron.
Caudron-clouter, tinker.
Corn, grain in general.
Cottar, cottager.
Cora Linn, a waterfall on the Clyde.
Cog, a small vessel.
Coupin', upsetting.
Chappit, knocked.
Chanter, part of the bagpipes.
Cleckit, hatched.
Clachan, (guttural,) hamlet.
Crap, crop.
Creel, hamper, large basket.
Crouse, glad, uplifted.
Craw, crow.
Crowlin', crawling.
Cuddie, donkey.

D.

Dee, die.
Dawin', dawning.
Daffin', laughing and jesting.
Dinnle, jar, slight shock.
Ding, knock.
Douce, sedate, respectable.
Dows, doves.
Duds, tatters.
Dyke, stone fence.

E.

Ee, eye.
Eeen, eyes.
Eild, old age.
Elshin, awl.
Eneuch, (guttural) enough.

F.

Fa', fall, lot, doom.
Fain, anxiously uneasy.
Faulding, folding.
Faun, fallen.
Fauts, faults.
Fell, dire, an open upland.
Fecht, (guttural) fight.
Fornent, opposite.
Forfoughten, wearied out.
Forgather, to meet with.
Forbears, ancestors.
Forrit, forward.
Forpit, the fourth part of a peck.
Fu', full (pron. foo.)

G.

Gae, go.
Gaed, went.
Gang, go.
Gaun, going.
Gar, compel.
Gey weel, pretty well.
Gear, treasure.
Gie, give.
Gin, (hard g) if.
Girn, a trap.
Girn'd, grinned.
Gied, gave.
Gien, given.
Glint, glance, sparkle.
Glib, talkative.
Glowered, stared.
Gloaming, twilight.
Gowan, wild daisy.
Gowd, gold.
Gowden, golden.
Gowdie-lane, a child able to walk alone.
Greet, weep.
Grat, wept.
Grewsome, forbidding, disgusted.
Guffaw, boisterous laugh.

H.

Ha', hall (pron. haw.)
Hame, home.
Harried, plundered.
Hained, husbanded.
Haud, hold.
Haughs, (guttural) bottom lands.
Howff, rendezvous.
Howkin', digging.
Hooly, carefully.
Hotched, hitched (with laughter.)
Hoodie-craw, carrion crow.

I.

Ingleside, fireside.
Ilk, *ilka*, each.
Ither, other.
Intill, into.

J.

"*Jethart's here?*" the battle-cry of Jedburgh.
Joukin, dodging.
Jousl't, jostled.

K.

Kail, soup.
Kent, *kenned*, knew.
Kirn-milk, buttermilk.
Kimmer, a familiar title for a woman or girl.
Knowe, knoll, small hill.

L.

Law, a hill.
Laverock, lark.
Leal, true-hearted.
Lear, (pron. lair) learning.
Lintie, linnet.
Lift, sky, atmosphere.
Limmer, hussy.
Links, the flats of a very winding river.
Lingle or *lingel*, a shoemaker's "waxed end."
Lilts, sings.
Lochs, (guttural) lakes.
Loons, fellows.
Loup, jump.
Lo'e, *lo'ed*, love, loved.
Lucky, a familiar title for a landlady or mistress.

M.

Maist, most.
Mak, make.
Mair, more.
Maun, must.
Mantin', imperfectly articulating.
Mattent, sprouting.
Min-e-wae, minuet.
Mirky, dark.
Minnons, minnows.
Mools, mould, clods.
Mou, mouth.
Muckle, much, big.
Mutch, woman's cap.

O.

O', of.
Ower, over.
Oobit, caterpillar.

P.

Parritch, porridge.
Pawkie, sly.
Pibroch, (guttural) a martial air on the bagpipes.
Pirn, spool.
Pouch, pocket.
Poortith, poverty.
Purling, softly murmuring.
Pu'in, pulling.

Q.

Quean, a young girl.

R.

Reamy, creamy.
Roupit, sold by auction.
Rowe, row.
Row't, rolled.

S.

Sair, sore.
Saut, salt.
Sark, the under garment.
Sax, six.
Scart, scratch.
Scaur, precipitous bank.
Sclates, slates.
Screed, portion, or shred.
Screevin', shouting.
Sic, *siccan*, such.
Sheiling, hut.
Shaw, wood or grove.
Souter, shoemaker.
Sough, (guttural) sigh, hollow sound.
Sowp, sup, mouthful.
Sudna, should not.
Snood, ribbon for the hair.
Spells, spelling lesson.
Stooks, shocks of grain.
Stoure, (lit. dust) strife.
Straught, (guttural) straight.
Steek, stitch, fastening.
Strath, broad open valley.

T.

Tawse, a strap, with several "tails," used by a schoolmaster.
Tether, fastening, leading string.
Theek, thatch.
Thegither, together.
Thairms, harp-strings.
Thoomb, thumb.
Thole, endure.
Town, farm-steading.
Toom, empty.
Twined, deprived.
Tryst, appointment.

U.

Unco, strange, strangely.

W.

Wa', wall (pron. waw.)
Wae, woe, sad.
Wat, wot, know.
Wad, would.
Wale, selection.
Waukers, fullers.
Wantin', lacking.
Wame, stomach, abdomen.
Wapinschaw, a gathering of all the fighting men of a district.
Wersh, tasteless, insipid.
Wi', with (pron. we.)
Wiss, *wuss*, wish.
Whilk, which.
Whinger, dagger or short sword.
Whangs, liberal slices.
Wyte, blame.
Whyte, whittle.

Y.

Yauld, nimble, athletic.
Yett, gate.
Yerkit, jerked.
Yird, earth.
Yowes, ewes.

JUST ISSUED

THE
Poems of William Wye Smi

Elegantly bound in Green and Gold: Portrait: 266 pp.:
Very fine Paper. $1.00.

Copies may be had of the Author, Rev. W. W. Smith, Newma
Ontario, free by post, on receipt of price, One Dollar.

See Recommendations, from leading citizens and the Press, on next pa

Recommendations and Opinions of the Press.

G. MERCER ADAM, ESQ., *Toronto.*

Rev. and dear Sir.—Pray accept my hearty thanks for your courtesy in sending me a copy of your collected verse. I need hardly say that it is a gratification to me to see the repeated evidences in Canada, that the Muses are b ing courted with ardor and effect. If our people would only be a little more appreciative of native work, and more actively recognize literature as a profession, and remunerate it, what should we not accomplish? I look forward with pleasure to a leisure hour, when I can read your attractive volume through. Meantime I know enough of your work to highly appreciate it, and to thank you in advance for the pleasure that is in store for me. With respect, very cordially yours,

G. MERCER ADAM.

REV. PRINCIPAL CAVEN, *Knox College, Toronto.*

My dear Sir—I thank you very much for your volume of poems which you have kindly sent me. Several of them have already been perused with sincere pleasure, which, I am sure, will be greatly increased when I shall have read more extensively.

It is truly pleasing to find the poetic Muse taking delight in the highest themes, and commending these both to the old and the young. Religion and poetry—as in your beautiful volume—should ever be friends. With best wishes and with compliments of the season, yours very truly,

WM. CAVEN.

REV. PRINCIPAL GRANT, *Queen's University, Kingston.*

My dear Sir.—Many thanks for the copy of your poems. I have only had time so far to glance over it. Your preface strikes the right key; and "Circe" is a fine interpretation of the old story. Your Canadian pieces too, have the right color and ring "Indian Summer" and "John Greenwood" seem to me typical pieces. Hoping to see you when you visit Kingston—and with kind New-Year's greetings—believe me, yours sincerely,

G. M. GRANT.

PRESIDENT DANIEL WILSON, *Toronto.*

I have to thank you for a copy of your volume of poems, which I have looked over with much pleasure. The Scottish pieces are full of allusions which awaken sympathetic feelings in me. . . . Accept my best thanks.

SIR WILLIAM DAWSON, *Montreal.*

I beg to thank you for your kind gift of your volume of poems, which I appreciate very much, and hope they will reach and teach many of our too prosaic Canadians. I fear I am myself too little gifted with the appreciation of poetic fire; but I can at least appreciate the fine spirit which breathes in the religious and patriotic pieces in your volume.

SIR A. CAMPBELL, LIEUT.-GOVERNOR, *Ontario.*

I thank you much for your attention in sending me a copy of your poems, which I will look over with interest. Truly Yours,

A. CAMPBELL.

HON. OLIVER MOWAT, *Premier of Ontario.*

Thanks for copy of your poems. I have read them with much pleasure. I congratulate you upon the poetic merit which they display. The patriotism of some of them is stirring to a lover of his country.

THOS. COWHERD, ESQ, *Brantford.*

A thousand thanks, my dear friend and brother, for your beautiful book! Beautiful outwardly and inwardly—beautiful spiritually and artistically. May your reward be as great as you deserve!

REV. PRINCIPAL BARBOUR, *Montreal.*

I find on my desk your kind remembrance of me, in the new volume of your poems. I at once return you my sincere thanks, and express great pleasure in my anticipated reading of the contents. . . . Let me again thank you for your beautiful book.

ADVERTISER, *London.*

Rev. W W. Smith, productions from whose pen have frequently made the columns of the *Advertiser* more interesting, has issued a volume of original poems. The poems are varied, many being written in response to Thos. MacQueen's plea, "Will nobody write a few songs for Canada?" Some are Scottish, many religious, while through others there is a deep vein of humor. We take pleasure in recommending the book, which is neatly printed and handsomely bound, to our readers.

GLOBE, *Toronto.*

Rev. Wm. Wye Smith, who is well known to the readers of the *Globe* as a racy writer, has published a volume of poems. The verses are full of the truest and tenderest feeling. The Canadian poems are instinct with patriotism, and his Scotch dialect work has the bloom of the heather upon it. A few deeply religious poems and delightful little nursery rhymes are also to be found in the book.

CANADA PRESBYTERIAN, *Toronto.*

There is nothing in this fine little volume to indicate the profession of the writer. Here he makes his appearance as a poet only. Mr. Smith is the respected minister of the Congregational Church, Newmarket. As a Canadian *litterateur* he is well and widely known. He now presents to the reading public a volume of excellent poems, ranging over a variety of subjects, such as miscellaneous, Canadian, Scotch, religious, psalms, children's pieces. These poems show that their author possesses the poet's inspiration and the gift of expression. The book deserves, and doubtless will meet, with a favorable reception.

MAIL, *Toronto.*

"Poems," by the Rev. William Wye Smith, Newmarket, Ont., is a neatly bound volume which brings together some lyrics whose acquaintance the reader of the "Poet's Corner" of several periodicals has already made, and many other productions from the author's pen which are now for the first time published. The publication of the book will add Mr. Smith's name to the widening circle of Canadian poets, to which he will be welcomed as no mean acquisition. The work consists of a series of short poems in the order of Miscellaneous, Canadian, Scottish, Religious, Psalms, and children's pieces, and over this range there are many evidences of ability in the poetic art. The chief merit of the work will be found in the children's pieces and in the Scottish verse. Indeed, the whole tenor of the book appeals to Scottish sympathy, and several poems are good specimens of the average Scottish muse. That the author is not ambitious in his design and keeps well within the limits of his unpretentious but pleasing muse, will in no small measure help his praiseworthy efforts.

ALEXANDER MCLACHLAN, ESQ., *Amaranth.*

My dear friend, I have received your volume for which please accept my warmest thanks. . . . I hope soon to have time to sit quietly down and give the volume the perusal it deserves. By the bye, do you think the portrait a good likeness? It seems to me that your face is too full. However, some of my family knew you at once.

CANADIAN ADVANCE *Toronto.—A Canadian Poet.*

The Rev. William Wye Smith, of Newmarket, whose portrait we give above, has placed on our table a copy of his poems recently issued from the press. It is a neatly printed and bound volume of 264 pages, and will prove a valuable addition to our native literature, which we are gratified to see is so rapidly extending and improving. Mr. Smith yields a facile and graceful pen, as evinced in his admirable prose sketches, and the present work will naturally add to his reputation in this respect. The contents exhibit a wide range of subjects, a goodly proportion of the poems being distinctively Canadian, as others are Scotttish in their lines. The large number, however, treat of religious subjects and hymns founded on the Psalms: while the children are remembered in a choice list of verses. . . . The poet is particularly happy in his Scottish pieces which breathe of the Heather and Broom.

THE WORLD, *Toronto.*

This is a collection of verses from the pen of Rev. W. W. Smith, of Newmarket It embraces poems on Canadian. Scottish, religious and miscellaneous, many of which are quite readable. We reprint one, "The Second Concession of Deer," in another column.

CHRISTIAN GUARDIAN, *Toronto.*

We have been familiar with Mr. Smith's poems for many years and are pleased to see this tasty volume, which contains doubtless what he himself likes best. . . . Many o these poems are full of tender poetic feeling fitly expressed in elegant and harmonious language. There is in the book considerabe variety of subjects, as they are divided into Miscellaneous, Canadian, Scottish, Religious, Paraphrases of Psalms, and Children's Poems. Mr. Smith sees the poetic side of common things.

SONG—INDIAN SUMMER.

The air is full of sunshine,
　The woods are full of dew;
The lake is like the distant sky,
　The sky has lost its blue.—
And flooded with a golden haze,
　All nature lies becalmed;
Like music in the memory,
　With loving thoughts embalmed.

　　Stay, stay, sweet Indian Summer!
　　　I grieve to have thee go!
　　O let thy smile be mine awhile,
　　　'Twixt the Autumn and the sn w!

The birds that round my window
　Their early matins sung,—
The flowers I watched each Summer eve,
　Till night its shadows flung;—
And gentle friends that came too late,
　And coming, went too soon—
These all pass o'er my memory
　Like shadows o'er yon moon.

Cho:

But Nature all is golden,
　Ev'n in her last decay;
And Hope, that saw its brighter hours,
　Will have a happier day.
And love, and friends to crown that love,
　I yet shall live to see;
Though darkness, distance, winter lies
　Between that hope and me!

Cho:

THE NURSE O' MEN.

O, mony a ane can whistle
　That could never guide the plow;
And Souters may turn Sailors,
　That can neither steer nor rowe;—
And a man may bear a Scottish name,
　And dwell in Scottish glen,
Yet never hae the hero-heart
　That maks him king o' men!

I might hae been rich, my Jeanie,
　Gin I had lived for gold!
There was mony a ane to purch se,
　Gin I my heart had sold!

But I kent it lay wi' Scotland's sons
　To tak auld Scotland's part;
And her dear name, and thy sweet love
　Were life-beats in my heart!

Though whiles frae the pirn o' Sorrow
　Comes Luve, the weft o' life,
Yet the sun will shine, my Jeanie,
　Though the mirky clouds sae rife!
And wha bides true to a' that's true
　Wins mair than gowden gear—
The balmy peace o' a heart at ease,—
　And hope and heaven sae near!

Fair gae they, and fair come they,
　That love auld Scotland weel!
Their waes gang in a forpit,
　Their guid come in a creel!
And aye the love that they may seek
　Be leal as that they gie,—
And in thy blessing, Nurse o' Men!
　Ilk son be bless d wi' thee!

THE MERITS OF CHRIST FOR NOTHING

The merits of Christ for nothing,
　Large, and white, and fair!
I am bidden to come to the Supper,
　And that is the robe I'll wear!
Woven in light—pure and white—
　A princely robe to bear;—
The merits of Christ for nothing,—
　Large, and white, and fair!

He'll honor the robe he gave me
　With his own royal hand;
And smile when he sees me enter
　As one of his ransomed band.
Children of light! clothed in white!
　As in your ranks I stand—
He'll honor the robe he gave me
　With his own royal hand.

The sweetest hope I have cherished
　In now to be saved by grace;—
That vainest of hopes has perished—
　Through works to see God's face!
The robe of Christ—his worth unpriced—
　Here all my trust I place;—
The sweetest hope I have cherished
　Is now to saved by grace!

www.ingramcontent.com/pod-product-compliance
Lightning Source LLC
Chambersburg PA
CBHW031947230426
43672CB00010B/2074